OTHER WORKS BY JOHN P. STRELECKY

The Why Café

Return to the Why Café

Ahas!

Life Safari

The Big Five for Life

How to be Rich and Happy (Co-author)

THE
BIG FIVE
for LIFE
CONTINUED

EXCITING TIMES

THE
BIG FIVE
for LIFE
CONTINUED

EXCITING TIMES

JOHN P. STRELECKY

ASPEN LIGHT PUBLISHING

Many of the designations used by manufacturers and sellers to distinguish their products are claimed as trademarks. Where those designations appear in this book and Aspen Light Publishing was aware of a trademark claim, those designations have been printed with initial capital letters.

Copyright © 2015 by John P. Strelecky

All rights reserved. No part of this publication may be reproduced, stored in a retrieval system, or transmitted, in any form or by any means, electronic, mechanical, photocopying, recording, or otherwise, without the prior written permission of the publisher.

Printed in the United States of America.

Publication Data:
Strelecky, John P.
The Big Five for Life - Continued / John P. Strelecky. 1st Aspen Light Publishing ed.

ISBN-13: 978-0-99139202-5

Published by Aspen Light Publishing
Inquiries to the author can be directed to:

John P. Strelecky c/o Aspen Light Publishing
13506 Summerport Village Parkway Suite #155
Windermere, FL 34786
The author can be reached through
www.bigfiveforlife.com

Message From the Author

SOMETIMES WONDERFUL THINGS HAPPEN IN WAYS you couldn't possibly plan. That's the case with the way this book came to be.

After one of my earlier books—*The Big Five for Life*—was published, I started receiving many emails from readers. Something in that story had touched a chord with people. Some of the messages were from individuals who wanted to say thank you for helping them think about their life in a new way.

Many were from leaders. They wanted to create cultures like the book described, and were asking for more details.

All were very inspiring.

Then one day, I received a message from a gentleman named Jacques Guénette. He shared that he had really enjoyed the book. So much so, that after reading it, he and his wife both took the time to determine their own Big Five for Life. He also shared that for the last thirty years he'd been running a company in the same spirit as what I'd described in the book.

This intrigued me greatly. I looked up where his company was located. Outside of Montreal, Canada. About a twenty minute drive from where I'd be doing a speaking event—in two weeks.

Coincidence? I didn't think so. I contacted Jacques and asked if we might spend a few minutes together when I was in Montreal. That "few minutes" ended up being two hours and the inspiration for this book.

In the following pages, you're going to meet Jacques and learn about his company—DLGL. That will occur through the continuation of the Big Five for Life story from my previous book. I realize this may be a touch confusing. Which parts of the story are "story" and which parts are not. So let me clarify that.

What you'll be reading about DLGL and Jacques— the awards, business practices, history, approach to leadership and life…. All of it is real. The happy moments and the sad. They've been incorporated into the continuation of the Big Five for Life story, because as you'll see—it was a perfect fit.

A perfect way to help the many leaders who have been asking for more details on creating Big Five for Life cultures in their organizations. A perfect way to help readers of all types, let go of what's holding them back.

And since sharing the DLGL story and being a part of writing a book are part of Jacques' personal Big Five for Life…it was perfect in that regard too.

Like I said, sometimes wonderful things happen in ways you couldn't possibly plan. And sometimes coincidences…aren't so coincidental. All of which you'll discover, in the pages ahead.

Enjoy!

Your fellow traveler,

John

Chapter 1

JOE WALKED TO THE LEFT SIDE OF THE STAGE AND paused for a moment. He had just shared a powerful story and was letting the message sink in. "Time to close," he thought.

He looked out at the audience, "While I don't know what is on each of your Big Five for Life lists, I do know this. If you take it one step at a time, one *moment* at a time, and you remain committed to the direction you know in your heart you want to go...wonderful things will happen. I promise you they will.

"Thank you very much ladies and gentlemen. It has been an honor to be with you here today."

The applause began almost instantly. Then people started standing. Joe nodded at the audience and put his right hand over his heart. It was a gesture to acknowledge and thank them for the standing ovation he was now getting.

In the wings of the stage, in an area behind a curtain, a woman was watching Joe. She could see him, and some of the audience, but neither could see her. She was watching Joe intently. Looking for a sign. A clue. Something which would tell her he was OK. Or maybe *not* OK.

The presentation had been marvelous. Joe had taken the audience on a wonderful emotional roller coaster ride. They had laughed, cried, and then felt their hearts soar through the inspirational story he told at the end. Through that story, and in particular because of the way Joe had told it, they connected with their own true potential for greatness.

Based on the audience reaction, it all looked OK. Far *better* than OK. She knew not to be fooled by that though. Joe was a great presenter. And this presentation he had given enough times he knew every word of it by heart.

As the applause began to die down, people from the event organizing team arranged microphones in the aisles so audience members could ask questions. The woman watched as someone stepped up to one of them.

"Why is it the Big Five and not ten or fifty or one hundred?"

Joe smiled, "Two reasons. The first is that..."

When he was done with the answer, another person stepped up to a microphone.

"What do you do once you've completed one of your Big Five for Life? Do you add another one or wait until you do the other four?"

Joe smiled again. These were questions he had been asked many times before. That was one of the beautiful aspects of the Big Five for Life. It was a concept so simple to understand and implement in one's life, that there were only a few core questions people seemed to have.

"That depends on the person," he began. "For some people..."

When Joe finished giving his explanation, the moderator for the event stepped to one of the microphones, "We have time for one more question."

Chapter 2

SO FAR, THE WOMAN WATCHING JOE HAD SEEN NO indication that anything was out of the ordinary. She glanced as a man from the audience made his way to one of the microphones in the isle. He would ask the final question of the night.

"How strange life is," she thought. It was just over a year ago when her whole life had been turned upside down. A year ago that the doctors had called and told her the person she loved more than anyone else in the world, was dying.

The memory made her sad. "I miss you, Thomas," she said silently.

She was here today, in part, because of Thomas. He had been Joe's mentor. Also his best friend. She and Joe were friends too. The three of them had gone on many adventures together. There had been a special bond between Thomas and Joe, though. Like a combination of best friends, father and son, mentor and protege.... It was the friend equivalent of what she and Thomas had as a couple.

When Thomas died, everyone around him took it hard. He'd only been fifty-five years old, and the illness had struck fast and harshly. Within months of being diagnosed, his life had ended.

Joe was there at the end. It was a tough time. Now, seven months had gone by. And day by day, it was getting easier for her. Not easy. Not even close to easy. But easier.

It was another phone call which brought her to where she was right now. This time from Kerry Dobsin. Kerry was the president of one of Thomas' companies. Part of Derale Enterprises. She and Kerry had known each other for a long time and had developed a deep friendship.

Kerry knew Joe, too. Their friendship wasn't as deep as what the two women had, but it was strong. And built upon a high degree of respect for who Joe was and what he brought to Derale Enterprises. It was because of that respect that she had called.

"It isn't something concrete," Kerry had said on the phone. "He's as inspiring as he's always been. He's funny and charming and connects with people just like always."

"But?"

"But something's different."

The woman's mind switched back to the present. The man from the audience was now at the microphone. "Hi, Joe. Thanks very much for your inspiring presentation."

Joe nodded in acknowledgement.

"My question really isn't about the presentation. It's about Thomas Derale. I'm just wondering who will replace him at Derale Enterprises?"

The woman saw it instantly. The flash of pain which passed across Joe's face. A moment later he had covered it with a smile. But she had seen it. The intense hurt was still there.

Joe coughed into his hand. An unconscious delay tactic. "Or maybe conscious," she thought.

"Thank you for your question," Joe said. He hesitated. His face went blank for a moment. "Derale Enterprises is full of talented, dedicated people," he said after a moment. "I know the organization will continue for a long time."

Joe glanced at his watch, "Thank you all again for choosing to be here tonight. It's been a wonderful event." His voice had returned to its normal energetic level. "I wish you all the success possible as each of you fulfills your own Big Five for Life. And also as you help others live theirs."

There was a loud round of applause and people stood once again.

The temporary energy shift from the last question hadn't impacted the room or dampened the effect of Joe's presentation. It was doubtful anyone in the audience even caught it.

But she had.

Chapter 3

JOE WAVED TO THE AUDIENCE, THEN TURNED AND headed for the side area of the stage. When he had been facing the audience, he'd been smiling. When he turned, his smile quickly faded.

She nodded to herself. Kerry had been right.

Although his eyes were open and he seemed to be looking straight ahead, Joe almost ran right into her as he walked toward the backstage exit.

"That was a great presentation, Joe," she said when he was right in front of her.

Joe stopped short and his mind snapped back from wherever it had been. His eyes focused.

"Maggie," he said warmly and smiled. He opened his arms and gave her a hug. "What a nice surprise."

She hugged him back.

"I haven't seen you much, Joe. How have you been?" she asked as they separated.

For just a second, his smile dropped again. She saw it, even though he quickly brought it back.

"Good," he replied. He shrugged, "It's been really busy." He hesitated, "I'm sorry I haven't been around much the last few months. I just...." His voice trailed off.

"It's OK," she replied. And it was OK. Maggie was fifteen years older than Joe. Those extra years had provided her with life experiences which helped her understand that different people grieve in different ways.

Maggie had reached out more to her friends. The social interactions had brought some solace. They had reminded her that although Thomas was gone, she had much to live for. Joe had done the opposite. On stage he was brilliant. In the office he was engaged and articulate. Beyond that, he had chosen isolation.

"Joe, I have a favor to ask." Maggie had planned her words carefully. She knew Joe wouldn't acknowledge his pain. And he wouldn't ask for help. But he was a giver, and if she asked him for his assistance…then through that path, she might be able to help him.

"Sure, Maggie. Anything. What is it?"

"Well, you know those profile pieces you do? Where you go spend time at companies with great leaders and great cultures and then do an article about them?"

Joe nodded. It wasn't something he did often, but when he learned of a really amazing company, he would invest his time with them. It gave him powerful material to share throughout the different companies which composed Derale Enterprises. It also gave him great stories when he was hosting the leadership summits each year. Those were when Derale Enterprises brought in their suppliers, customers, and partners to a huge event where they shared new ideas.

"I'd like you to consider doing one about a friend of mine," Maggie said. "He's up in the Montreal, Canada area. His name is Jacques Guénette and he runs a company called DLGL."

Joe nodded, "OK. I'll look them up." He paused for a moment, "Any particular reason for doing this now?"

Maggie nodded back and smiled, "Well, the first reason is Jacques has decided to semi-retire. I was catching up with him on the phone last night and he mentioned it. So he's going to be less available at his company. Equally important for you though, is that it's the end of June now. Which means Montreal has probably finally hit a warm enough temperature where you'd consider going."

Joe smiled. His intolerance for cold weather was well known among his friends. "And will probably be so cold in another couple of months I won't want to go," he added.

Maggie returned the smile. "*Exactly*," she said with emphasis.

"Sure," Joe said. "If you send me his contact information I'll reach out to him. I'm pretty booked for the next few weeks, but I can probably get up there mid-July if he's available then."

"Great." Maggie opened her arms and hugged Joe. She kissed him on the cheek.

"He's a great guy," she said when they parted. "You'll like each other."

Chapter 4

JOE WAS ALONE IN HIS APARTMENT. THE TELEVISION was on, but he wasn't paying attention to it. His phone rang and he glanced at it. Sonia. He hit a button and sent the call to voicemail. "Sorry," he said. "Just not in the mood to talk." He hoped she understood.

Joe had met Sonia on a flight back from Europe almost a year earlier. It was right after he learned Thomas was dying. Sonia and Joe had clicked on a lot of levels. She had even gone with him and Thomas to an event at Derale Enterprises. But when Thomas died, Joe had distanced himself. It just didn't feel the same.

Another time, different circumstances, it might have turned into something. Not now.

Joe's phone beeped. He glanced at it again. It was a text from Maggie. "Just sent you Jacques' contact information and the company website. Thx. Go soon or pack your winter jacket :)"

Joe felt bad about that relationship too. He knew Maggie was hurting. That Thomas' death was very hard on her. They had been married for thirty-one years and it had been one of those truly great love affairs. Thomas had loved her with all his heart and Maggie had felt the same.

The three of them had been on many adventures together. Sometimes just them, other times with Joe bringing whoever he was dating. He and Maggie were good friends. So why was it so hard to see her now? He didn't know. And he felt bad for not being able to be there for her.

Something had changed in Joe when Thomas died. He had never experienced the death of someone close to him before. His parents were still alive, and when his grandparents passed it hadn't meant much because he didn't know them very well.

This was different. This was his best friend. And it had hurt. It still hurt. When he thought of Thomas, or someone else brought him up, Joe's mind would slip into a dark place. A depressing place. And he couldn't figure out how to make the pain or the darkness go away.

He was the guy who helped other people. He was good at that. But he couldn't help himself on this one. And because of that, he didn't feel like he could help Maggie or anyone else deal with it either.

Joe picked up his phone and clicked on the contact Maggie had sent. Jacques Guénette. DLGL. Human Resource Software. "Not the type of industry which typically gets people all excited," he thought to himself. But he knew better than that. In the last decade since joining Thomas' company, he had been given the chance to meet amazing leaders from all walks of life.

They came in all shapes and sizes and worked in all types of organizations. When you're good, you're good, he had learned. And if it interests you, you can build a great company in any industry.

One of his favorite interviews had been with a baker in the Netherlands—Klaes Hoekstra. Joe had known nothing about baking and wasn't sure what he would encounter when he met Klaes. What he found was a vibrant man, with eyes full of life, and a spirit for adventure.

Klaes lived in a village called Badem, in the northern part of the Netherlands. Just over nine-thousand people lived there, and in a given week, one third of all the men, women, and children in the village would come to his bakery. He had created something that special.

Joe turned and scanned the bookshelf behind him. He smiled when he saw what he was looking for. "World Famous...in Badem." That was the title of the book Klaes had written. It always made Joe laugh when he read it. "World Famous...in Badem."

Joe reached for the book and pulled it off the shelf. He opened it. Even the book was full of spirit and energy. It was loaded with pictures and stories from the thirty years Klaes had been in business.

Klaes connected with people. He really did. He made you feel important and special when you were with him. Joe had seen him create that atmosphere with customers, with the people who worked at the bakery.... "A good guy," Joe thought. "And a heck of a leader."

Joe was about to shut the book, but he stopped at the first page as he was about to close the cover.

Klaes had written an inscription in the book. "Everyone is special. Helping people remember that is what we both do. You in your way, and me in my bakery." He had signed it—Klaes.

Joe shut the book. The last time he'd spoken with Klaes had been almost a year and a half ago. At the time, Klae's wife of forty-two years, had just died of cancer. Klaes was struggling to find himself. Struggling to find the same meaning in things that used to feel so meaningful.

At the time, Joe couldn't quite relate to that. He could now.

Chapter 5

"HOW WAS HE?" KERRY ASKED.

Maggie took a sip from her tea cup. After attending the event and talking with Joe, she had set up a time for this conversation with Kerry. Kerry needed to know.

"He's Joe," Maggie said and smiled.

Kerry nodded. "I can't say I'm able to understand how hard this is for you," she said. "You know we all loved Thomas." She shook her head, "Most of us worked with him for such a long time and had so many laughs and such great memories.... And then he's just gone. And you want to hang onto him. But he's still gone."

Maggie nodded.

"But I know that's probably nothing compared to what it's been like for you. And I know it's been tough for Joe to deal with too. They were such great friends."

Maggie nodded again.

"It's just that something is going to happen," Kerry said. "The board members want to allow everyone to take time. Not that we don't understand."

Maggie held up her hand slightly, "You don't have to apologize, Kerry. I own my own company. I understand that at some point someone needs to take Thomas' position."

"And people want it to be Joe," Kerry added. "I don't want you to think that isn't the case. As you know, Thomas' role was to connect people from his different companies. And to be the visionary for new companies and new things to bring to all of us…."

She hesitated, "Joe is the right guy for that. Not just because he and Thomas were so close in the way they thought and acted. Or that he knows and embraces the spirit of the culture Thomas created. Also for all the things that make him uniquely Joe, too."

Kerry looked away, "It's just that…,"

"People are worried he isn't quite him anymore," Maggie interjected quietly.

Kerry nodded.

"Does he even want the job?" Maggie asked.

"I don't know. Each time I've brought it up, he always says it's too soon to even be talking about it. He says he knows there needs to be a change at some point, but not yet."

Kerry shrugged, "Our last few conversations have ended about the same way. He asks me to give him a few weeks to think things over, or finish up something he's working on…. Then I don't hear from him.

"And I guess that's part of what the concern is too. We don't want to offer him the role if he isn't there mentally. And we don't want to offer it if he doesn't really want it, only to have him take it out of a sense of obligation to us, or to…" she hesitated.

"Out of a sense of obligation to Thomas," Maggie said.

Kerry nodded again.

"How much longer are you and the other board members willing to wait?"

"We feel things will really start slipping across the organizations if someone doesn't start filling this gap in the next sixty days. It's been seven months already."

Kerry reached across the table and put her hand on Maggie's, "I'm sorry, Maggie. I don't want to burden you with this when you're going through your own grieving and letting go process. I didn't know who else to turn to though. You know, Joe. We do too. You know him outside the world of Derale Enterprises though. I thought that would help."

"It's OK," Maggie replied. "It's not a burden. It's about helping a friend." She looked away for a moment, "Give me a month," she said. "After seeing Joe at the event, I put something into motion. Give that a chance to evolve a little bit and then let's talk again."

She looked at Kerry, "To be honest, if it doesn't work, then I don't think Joe is the right guy for the position."

Kerry nodded, "Then I hope it works."

Chapter 6

JACQUES GLANCED UP AT THE CLOCK IN HIS OFFICE. The meeting would start in an hour. He had time to answer a few emails.

He logged into his account. "Maggie Derale," he said quietly as his eyes scanned the new messages in his inbox. "I wonder what that's about."

He clicked the message and quickly read what it said. Then he nodded slowly. Instinctively he glanced up at the large picture on the wall. It was a photo of Claude Lalonde, the man who had co-founded DLGL with Jacques over thirty years earlier.

Jacques reached for the keyboard and typed. "Send him up. I'll do what I can. You are in Diane and my thoughts." He signed it—"Jag".

Jag was how he was known throughout his company. It was an acronym for Jacques Guénette. Over time it had become more than an acronym, it had become the way many people addressed him.

He liked it. Clean, simple, direct. That was his approach to most things in life and it worked well for this too.

Jacques pushed back from his desk. There were other emails he wanted to address, but his mind was on Maggie's message now. It brought back a flood of memories. "Life is strange like that," he thought. "You can be in the midst of something. Fully engaged in it. Then in an instant, a single thought, or word, can take you back to a part of your past."

He glanced up at Claude's picture again. "Maybe we can help this kid, eh Claude," he said. "And maybe Maggie too."

Chapter 7

JOE PULLED INTO THE PARKING LOT OF DLGL. TWO weeks had passed since he had first spoken with Maggie about doing the interview. Now here he was.

"Gotta love GPS," he thought to himself. He had never been in this part of Montreal before. He hadn't been to Canada all that much, and with Quebec being mostly French speaking, it added another layer of complexity for him.

The drive had been easy though, thanks to the GPS. And now he was about to meet Jacques Guénette, the leader Maggie had told him about.

Jacques had been very accommodating when Joe reached out via email and inquired about getting together. Joe knew Maggie was partially responsible for that. Still, he sensed it was also a large part of who Jacques was.

Joe had done his research on DLGL. They had an amazing track record. They'd won every award offered in their country for things like "Best Place to Work" and "Best Employer." For each of the last thirteen years they had been awarded the "Best Employer in the Province Award." For the last fifteen years, they were honored as part of the 50 Best Managed Companies. And they'd earned the #1 Best

Workplace in all of Canada award a number of times too, including for the current year.

Those kinds of results didn't come by accident. Joe knew from experience that they came from great leadership at the top and great people throughout.

When he was doing his research, Joe had noticed that the company's Mission and Philosophy were prominently displayed on the front page of their website.

That demonstrated clarity of purpose, which Joe had found to be one of the consistent themes throughout all the great companies he'd interacted with. After all, if you don't know who you are, where you're going, and the way you're going to act along the way, what chance do you have of actually arriving?

Joe pulled into a parking spot. He gathered his papers and computer bag. One of the papers was a printout of that front page of the DLGL website. He glanced at it.

Our Mission
Specialization in the conception, implementation and support of sophisticated, integrated, Human Resources, Payroll, Workforce Management, Pension, Talent Management, and Self-Service Portal systems, using high quality, proven, industry standard tools, with a total commitment to quality before volume."

Our Philosophy
*Quality of life
  -for employees
  -for clients
  -for shareholders

-for suppliers
*Quality of products before volume of business
*Profitability is the key to stability and quality
*A strong financial structure is required for perspective in decisions
*Software only
*Highly specialized in HRIS only
*Management by presumption of competence and honesty
*Best available industry standard tools
*Dealing with large employers
*Delivering the goods 100% of the time

Our Credo
"If DLGL serves the real best interests of its clients, the long term interests of DLGL will also be served."

Joe had learned over the years that you could tell a lot about people from the words they used. He'd learned to quickly spot patterns and trends when people spoke and also when they wrote. Those patterns and trends were a direct reflection of the people's beliefs. About themselves, about the world…. Those beliefs then resulted in the ways they acted.

When he'd first read the DLGL material, three things had stood out to Joe. He'd actually circled them on the printout. "Quality" and "Best" were used repeatedly. Clearly that was a focus for Jacques and DLGL. Not just in reference to what they offered as a product either. It was about quality of life too.

Client focused was a big pattern too. They had chosen to build their business with a client centric model. Their credo said it all.

"If DLGL serves the real best interests of its clients, the long term interests of DLGL will also be served."

The last thing Joe had noticed was the element of clarity and focus and the confidence with which it was articulated. The team at DLGL knew who they were, and equally important, who they weren't. And they weren't afraid to say it, which meant they knew they could deliver on it.

Joe put the papers into his bag and opened the car door. He smiled, "This should be interesting."

Chapter 8

AS JOE WALKED THROUGH THE DOOR INTO DLGL, HE noticed the degree to which the words he'd picked up on from the website, were reflected in the DLGL offices. Joe had interviewed leaders in all kinds of places. From two guys in a garage, to fancy offices in shimmering skyscrapers.

Each had a feel. An energy. So did this. It was professional and comfortable at the same time. Classy, but not in a throw it in your face way. There was wood everywhere. Real wood. And there was space. It felt like walking into a fine, established hotel, or country club.

Joe glanced back out the door and noted how well manicured the lawn was. He saw the walkway was pavers instead of just concrete. He'd felt a certain energy outside when he was walking up to the building. Now he noticed with more appreciation what had created the feeling. It was an orderliness blended with an appreciation for the beautiful. Even in things like the walkway and the lawn.

Joe returned his gaze to the inside and was immediately drawn to the pictures on the wall. They were from annual events where everyone in the company had gathered for something special.

In one, the people were on a large boat. In another, they were dressed in formal clothes and standing in a beautiful ballroom. Each picture had a year marked on the bottom.

One thing Joe saw immediately was that the people in the pictures were genuinely smiling. It was interesting how you could tell when things were genuine and when they weren't. You can't fake authentic happiness, which is what was in the pictures.

Joe passed through a second door and walked up to a reception desk. He immediately noticed the plaque on the desk—Director of First Impressions. "Quite a coincidence," Joe thought to himself. That title was something used in Derale Enterprises too.

The woman behind the desk smiled, "Good morning. Welcome to DLGL. Can I help you?"

"A good first impression," Joe thought. He smiled back at the woman, "Good morning. I'm here to see Jacques Guénette."

The woman smiled again, "Mr. Pogrete, correct?"

Joe nodded, "Yes."

She motioned toward some chairs, "Please have a seat and I'll let Jacques know you're here. Can I get you anything to drink?"

Joe shook his head, "I'm fine. Thank you."

The woman nodded and then picked up her phone and called someone. Joe looked around. The office was filled with outside light. He'd noticed the quantity of window space when he'd first glanced at the building from the outside. Now that he was inside, he realized they weren't just for aesthetics. All those windows had an important function. They allowed incredible amounts of natural light to come into the building.

"Joe, welcome to DLGL."

Joe turned in the direction of the voice. Approaching him was a man about six feet tall. He was wearing a dark blue polo style shirt with a logo Joe recognized as the logo for DLGL's main product. The man looked to be in his mid fifties. He had grey hair and light blue eyes which were both intense and friendly at the same time.

Joe smiled, "Jacques?"

The man smiled back, "Yes sir." He extended his hand and Joe shook it.

"Glad you could make it, Joe. How was your trip?"

"Good, thanks. Easy."

Jacques motioned to his left, "Come on, let's head to my office."

Joe followed him into a large office with lots of windows.

"Can I get you something to drink, Joe?"

"I'm fine, thanks."

"Then have a seat, please."

The two men sat down and faced each other.

"Thanks again for taking time to do this," Joe said. "As I mentioned in my email, I learned about you and your company through Maggie Derale."

"I spoke with her again last night," Jacques said. "She says you're a great guy and a heck of a traveler."

Joe smiled. Jacques had a deep booming voice which on its own might have seemed intimidating. Somehow though, the combination of the man and the voice had the opposite effect. It was comforting somehow.

"She also said you're passionate about helping people," Jacques added.

"I do my best," Joe replied.

"How do you know Maggie?" Jacques asked.

Joe paused for a moment, "Her husband, Thomas, was my mentor and my best friend. I met Maggie through him. I like to do adventure travel, so over the years I took the two of them to some of my favorite adventure places. Africa, Australia, Thailand...."

Jacques knew all this. Maggie had filled him in when she'd first called. Jacques wanted to hear it from Joe, though. He was looking for clues.

"And you?" Joe asked. "How do you know Maggie?"

"Through my wife, Diane," Jacques replied. "They met each other at school and always kept in touch. They like to do a girls trip every couple of years. So I've gotten to know her when she's been up here."

Joe nodded.

"So," Jacques said. "What do you have in mind for your time here? How can I help you?"

"Well, without being an imposition on you, I'd like to get to know you and DLGL. The project I'm working on is a series of interviews and profiles with great leaders from different types of organizations. I've been doing these for a number of years now. When each one is complete, I make it available to people within our companies and to our partners as well.

"I've found that great leaders tend to be life-long learners. So my goal is to bring at least five to ten thought provoking concepts or practices to them through each interview. Something they can read and then where appropriate, put to use in their own organization.

"This isn't something we charge others for. It's just our way of helping our own leaders grow, and our partners too."

Jacques nodded, "And how can I help you get to know us? What have you done at other places?"

Joe smiled, "Each interview tends to be a little different. Sometimes I've just sat with a leader for an hour or so and talked. That's it. Then I've taken that information and written it up."

Jacques smiled, "I can tell from your smile there's been others that are *way* more than that."

Joe nodded, "Well, the sit down conversation is one end of the spectrum..."

"And the other end?"

Joe smiled again, "Two years ago I worked in a bakery for three weeks, shadowing the owner so I could really tell his story."

Jacques nodded appreciatively, "Really?"

"Really."

"Was it worth it?"

"It was non-stop fun for three weeks. Even having to get up at four-thirty in the morning each day couldn't put a damper on it."

Joe leaned forward in his chair, "Jacques, I enjoyed reading through your website. You've obviously created a special place here. Seems like you've won pretty much every award available for best place to work. And on top of that, Maggie raved about what you've created. If an hour of conversation is best for you, let's do that. But my instincts tell me this is more of a 'bakery' scenario.

"Again, I don't want to inconvenience you. But if I could shadow you for a while. Immerse myself in the DLGL culture.... I think this would end up being a life-changing interview for a lot of leaders."

Jacques leaned back in his chair. He nodded and paused for a few moments, "Then that's what we'll do."

Chapter 9

JACQUES STOOD UP, "I'LL TELL YOU WHAT, JOE. WE'VE got a couple hours left in the day. Let's go for a walk around the place. Get you familiar with what we do. After that, you can come back and spend as many days as you'd like here.

"My schedule will be pretty busy these next two weeks. In addition to the regular things, I've got an interview with *Excellence*, which is a business magazine here in Montreal. We were just named the 'Best Place to Work' in all of Canada, and they'd like to learn more about us.

"Then a week from today I'm speaking at a conference on recruiting the best possible talent for corporations. You're welcome to join me for as much or as little of that as you want."

Joe stood up, "Probably all."

Jacques nodded and smiled, "All it is then."

"How long have you been in this building?" Joe asked as he and Jacques walked out of Jacques' office.

"We built this place almost twenty years ago. At first it was just this section. Then as we grew, we added more space in the back."

"Did you design it yourself? It has a great feel to it."

Jacques nodded and laughed, "Yeah the architects *loved* me. Right from the start I told them I wanted the most window space per person they could design. And in our next meeting, they came back with a design with hardly any windows.

"Their explanation was that it would cost a lot to do what I wanted. So I explained to them again that I wanted the most window space per person they could design."

He turned to me, "After the third time of them coming back with something I didn't want and justifying it by telling me how much they would save me, I finally had to tell them I was going to fire them unless they did what I asked."

Joe laughed, "And did they finally get it?"

"Yeah, after that meeting they finally got it as far as the windows were concerned."

"Well it definitely has a great feel to it. I noticed right when I came in how much natural light there is."

Jacques nodded, "This is where people spend the majority of their awake time every day. You don't want them sitting under fluorescent bulbs that blink a million times a minute and give them headaches. You don't want them staring at nothing but walls all day.

"That's inhuman. Not to mention it's a crummy way to optimize what you do every day. Can you imagine? People sitting someplace with constant headaches, their energy is low.... How can you ask them to effectively serve their clients if that's the atmosphere you put them in?"

"Did you help design the interior too?" Joe asked.

Jacques nodded again, "The same logic applied. We wanted to make it a special place. Professional, comfortable.... I had a similar discussion with the architects about the floors as I had with the windows. I told them I wanted wood. They told me it was too expensive. I told them I wanted wood. They told me it would wear out too fast. So at the third meeting about the flooring, I told them I wanted wood and if they came back with anything but what I wanted, I'd fire them."

Joe was starting to get a feel for Jacques' personality. He was direct, no doubt about it. His directness was with intention though, and it came from a desire to create something special for the people around him. He was a thinker too. Which meant when he arrived at a decision, it wasn't a random decision. He had thought about it at length and from a dozen different angles.

He was funny too. Even during their short time together, Joe had already noticed that when Jacques explained things and told stories, he had a natural way of demonstrating the irony in them. He made you laugh.

Chapter 10

"HOW MUCH DO YOU KNOW ABOUT THE BUSINESS we're in?" Jacques asked as they walked.

"Well, it's not my specific area of expertise, so not a whole lot. In looking through your website and some things I found online, I understand you provide software and then support of that software to large companies. All in the area of things like payroll, scheduling, pensions, talent management...."

Jacques nodded, "That's true. We specialize in HR software and we service large clients. Which summarizes things at about the one hundred thousand foot level. Far more interesting though, is when you dig down a little and start to understand what that really means and why it matters."

Jacques turned the corner. The two men were now standing in front of a row of clocks. He pointed to one. "That's the eastern time zone clock. Every day in Toronto, eight thousand nurses go on call to help patients at all the university hospitals. For the last seventeen years, our systems have provided those schedules. Making sure every nurse knows which shift they are on and where they are working.

"In those same hospitals, everyone likes to get paid. Which means some system needs to be able to keep track of how many hours each person worked, how much they make per week, did they go on vacation, did they work overtime, how much do they get if they did work overtime.... We do that too.

"All of those functions, and about thirty more, happen constantly throughout every day of every year for that client. And they happen flawlessly."

Jacques paused, "Because if they don't, patient's lives could be in jeopardy. You can't have people showing up at incorrect locations, or wrong times, when those people are nurses in hospitals. That's how important this is."

"And all of that is done through your system?" Joe asked.

Jacques nodded, "Correct. It's called VIP."

He moved over to another of the clocks. "This is a different time zone. Over here you have a mining operation in Manitoba. We're providing and exchanging real time information to people four thousand feet *underground*. Enabling them to make the best decisions about who does what, where, and when, as they run their operations.

"And over here," he said and indicated a third time zone, "we're providing our services to an urban community of more than half a million people. Things like schedules for firemen, pensions for employees, management of everyone's benefits."

Jacques turned and looked at Joe, "We supply our clients with all the tools they need to manage the complete relationship between the organization and its employees.

"That includes new hire candidate recruitment and selection, on-boarding, payroll, benefits, scheduling, training, competencies tracking, succession planning, retirement plans, and payments of benefits to the families of employees who pass away. For a single person, that whole sequence might encompass seventy years of their life."

Joe nodded.

"Our Purpose for Existence is to help our clients successfully fulfill *their* Purpose for Existence. It's something we take great pride in being a part of."

Chapter 11

THE TWO MEN WALKED THROUGH A SECTION OF the building where there were offices and common space. The outside light provided ample illumination for the entire area.

Joe motioned toward the space, "This has such a great feel to it."

Jacques smiled, "You create a place people enjoy being at and are proud to be a part of, and that shows up in the way they approach what they do every day. It also shows up in how long they stay with you. Our industry has an annual turnover rate of twenty percent. We have zero."

Joe nodded. Despite the huge costs of losing good people, the majority of organizations had to replace significant quantities of their work force every year. A zero percent turnover rate was almost unheard of—even in great companies.

As they walked, Joe noticed Jacques was greeted by whoever they passed. He in turn greeted them. It wasn't a fake "hello" either. There was a camaraderie to the brief interactions.

Earlier in his career, Joe had worked in a number of organizations where the leaders created command and control cultures. It was all based on fear. The result was that everyone was afraid to talk to the leader. Even people's physical stature would change when the leader was around. They would make themselves smaller.

This was clearly the opposite of that. People laughed with Jacques. They joked.

Joe asked Jacques about it.

"It's really pretty easy to treat people like people instead of trying to demonstrate how important you are all the time," he replied. "And the thing is, when you treat people well, they respond in kind."

The men were passing a row of conference rooms. Joe noticed they had plaques outside of them, which showed the name of the room.

"Are these the names of your clients?" he asked.

Jacques chuckled, "Yeah they get a kick out of that. They like to kid me that they paid for that room."

The men entered a wide passageway between two areas of the building. It was beautiful. Huge windows went all the way up to the ceiling, and the outside light reflected off the wood floors. The view through the windows was of a grassy courtyard and then the forest beyond.

Jacques stopped and pointed outside, "If you feel like a little hike in the woods while you're here, feel free. There are some trails out back there. People regularly walk them after lunch, or just to take a break. There's also a dozen mountain bikes in the basement. You're welcome to use those if you prefer that to walking."

Joe nodded.

"Or if the weather's not great, there's a driving range downstairs too," Jacques added. "Clubs and balls and everything you need are down there."

He started walking again.

"What's that?" Joe asked as they made it to the mid-point of the passageway.

There was a real tree in a giant pot. The tree was about eight feet tall and hanging from its branches were dozens of notes.

Jacques smiled, "That's a very precious tree. An *invegetation* of the relationship we want with our clients."

Joe chuckled at the made up word.

"Our business model is based on client intimacy," Jacques continued. "Which means deeply understanding our client's needs. Part of our process is that the client project team comes to our offices for final integration testing of the software we're about to deliver."

He shrugged, "Depending on the complexity of what was created, it can take days, or even months to test and make all the changes.

"That tree is from the team at Loto Quebec. They were a *very* complex delivery. They're in lots of businesses—lotteries, casinos, hotels, restaurants.... They've got lots of nuances too—multi-sites, multi-unions, high security requirements....

"Their team spent a couple of months here. Living with us, testing, bicycling.... When they left, they gave us this tree, and from the branches were all these handwritten messages. Thank you notes, farewell messages, memories."

Jacques looked at Joe, "Every time I walk by that tree, I smile. The way their people and ours connected was amazing. They became a single group dedicated to a common goal, and in the end, delivered an awesome product. And that's what it's all about."

He nodded, "On average, our clients have been with us for thirteen years. Some coming up on *twenty*. The story behind that tree is a good example of why that's the case. It's also a great daily reminder for all of us to keep that same spirit present in all we do."

Chapter 12

JACQUES TURNED A CORNER AND HE AND JOE entered a small foyer area near a stairwell. Even the stairwell was designed in a professional and stylish look.

"This is our stump," Jacques said and pointed to a large wooden stump on wheels. "We have an event where everyone who achieves their ten year anniversary with the company gets a chance to give a ten minute speech. And earn five hundred dollars per minute in the process."

Joe smiled, "What do you mean?"

Jacques returned the smile, "It started off as a way to reward people. After they hit the ten year mark, they are eligible for a five thousand dollar bonus. Which they earn by giving their ten minute stump speech.

"We used to hold it outside, and whoever's turn it was would stand on this big dead stump out in the grass. As we grew and decided to add on to the building, we needed the space where the stump was. So we had it dug up and preserved in epoxy so it would last forever." He smiled, "And we put wheels on it so we could move it around.

"So now, when we have someone hitting ten years, we host a big event here in the company and we roll in the stump and people get their chance."

Jacques nodded, "Those stump speeches are really emotional things. Funny. Heartfelt. Filled with memories and laughter. After every one, we say they can't possibly get better, and yet every time they do."

On the wall behind the stump were large banners, about eight feet tall and three feet wide. There was a ten year banner, a fifteen year, and a twenty year. The names of the people who had been at DLGL for that long were on them along with their picture.

Joe looked at the banners. Clearly this was an organization which focused on the long term. It was also an organization that honored tradition.

Jacques motioned towards the stairs, "Let's head up."

They made their way to the third floor of the building. Jacques opened the door and they entered a massive workout facility. It was at least six thousand square feet. There were weights, workout machines, treadmills, space for yoga and aerobics.... It was state of the art.

Instead of being brick or concrete, the walls were all windows. So just like in the lower floors, natural light flooded in.

"This is all part of DLGL?" Joe asked surprised.

Jacques nodded, "Welcome to the Vipnasium. In addition to all the equipment you see, we have a personal trainer who's here full time. Each employee has a personal workout plan she helped design for them."

He nodded towards a young woman across the room, "That's her. I'll introduce you."

"Raquel, I'd like you to meet someone. This is Joe," Jacques said as they approached the woman. She smiled and extended her hand, "Hi Joe."

Joe shook her hand.

"Joe's going to be with us for a while. He's working on an interview about some of the things we do here at DLGL."

"What percent of the people use this facility and your help?" Joe asked.

"Over the course of the year I'll work with one hundred percent of the people. On a daily basis, forty-four percent of them come in. I teach yoga classes every day around the lunch hour and other group classes at other times of the day. Then a lot of personal training sessions in and around all of those."

Joe looked around. It was the middle of the afternoon and there were three or four people lifting weights. "People can work out anytime during the day?"

Jacques nodded, "Or night. Everyone has a passcode for the building. They can come and go twenty-four hours a day. That way they can use the facilities when they want. Not just here, but anything in the building."

"Does it ever get too crowded for you to help people?" Joe asked Raquel.

She shook her head, "No. Since people can come and go whenever they want, it's easy to plan my personal training sessions so everyone gets the help they want. If we forced people into little time slots, like only after five o'clock, it would be a problem. And to be honest, if we did that, we wouldn't have one hundred percent participation.

"But this way, people aren't forced to choose between family time, work responsibilities, and working out. Since they can structure it all how *they* want, they find the best way to fit it all in."

Raquel looked out across the room and saw a woman enter through the door. "That's my three-thirty client," she said and smiled. "I'm helping her prepare for a half-marathon. Do you guys have any other questions?"

"Dozens," Joe replied, "but I don't want to interrupt you. Can I come by some other time?"

"Absolutely. Come up and use the equipment too. Or join one of the classes."

Raquel patted Jacques on the shoulder and started walking toward her client. "See you, Jacques."

"Thanks, Raquel."

Jacques started walking towards the far end of the workout area.

"She seems great," Joe said.

Jacques nodded, "She is. It's been a great match."

"In what way?"

"She was a personal trainer at a commercial gym for a number of years, but got frustrated by it. People would sign up over the holidays, or when there was some marketing campaign, but then they kept dropping off. So it was tough to do what she wanted, which was to really help people get more fit.

"Eventually, she got so frustrated by it she quit and went into Human Resource work at a big company. Lucky for her and lucky for us, she spotted an ad we ran when we were looking to hire someone for this job. Now she's back doing what she loves, and working with people who are dedicated and available."

"How often is she here?"

"Eight to four, Monday through Friday. People can log onto her calendar through our intranet and get on her schedule for their personal training sessions. Or if someone has a stiff neck, or back, or some emergency, they can use her services for that too. She's a massage therapist as well as a trainer."

"What made you pick her out of the other applicants?" Joe asked.

Jacques smiled, "Well, she had all the important credentials we wanted in a trainer. Also, she was nice. And when she told us her story and said she was looking for the opportunity to do the job *right*…that was a big thing. Doing things right is a big piece of the way we operate." Jacques shrugged, "And it has worked out well. She's happy, we're happy…. A great fit."

Chapter 13

AS THEY WERE WALKING OUT, JACQUES MOTIONED toward an outside area on the roof, "Let's head out there for a moment."

They walked through the doors and out into a very pretty seating area. There were wood benches and latticed walls which provided shade and cover.

The area had a great view of both the courtyard below and the forests beyond. There were flowers everywhere.

"Beautiful," Joe said as he stopped and looked around.

"Thanks," Jacques replied. "This place and the courtyard down there are pretty popular spots at lunchtime, or when people want to get outside for a meeting."

"Whoever created it did a nice job," Joe said. "It's got a great feel to it."

"Actually, the people here at DLGL did it all," Jacques said. "After regular work hours, on weekends...."

"Really? What inspired them to take time away from their families and hobbies to do something like this?"

"People want to be part of something, Joe. This place is their second home. The people they work with are like a second family.

When you really think about it, if you take out the hours people are sleeping, they probably spend more time here than they do at home.

"When you give good people the opportunity to do good things, and provide them with the resources to make it happen—they do good things.

"For these types of endeavors, the company pays for all the supplies. Then people create what they want. Most of the employees participate. Not because they *have* to. They just *want* to. And it ends up being a great bonding experience for everyone too."

Jacques looked around for a few moments, "Come on," he said. "Let's show you the rest of the place."

Chapter 14

AS THEY STARTED WALKING, JOE TURNED TO Jacques, "Do people tend to work more hours here because you give them so much flexibility?"

Jacques shook his head, "I don't want people working more than 35-37 hours per week. They submit time sheets online where they list the hours they worked and the categories for where they spent their time. That helps make sure no one is feeling pressure to put in extra hours to get the job done."

Joe nodded, "Interesting."

"We use it in other ways too," Jacques said. "It helps us see what we're spending our time on as an organization. So if all of a sudden we're doing more support work than usual for a particular client, we'll see that right away. Or if something is taking longer in development than we projected, we'll see that too. It enables us to see potential issues forming, and take care of them, before they turn into real issues."

Joe nodded and wrote a few quick notes.

"In terms of people's individual schedules, everyone picks the hours they want to work," Jacques continued. "So if someone wants to do more one day, and less another, that's up to them."

"What do you do if a client tries to put pressure on someone to get something done right away?"

Jacques shook his head, "If something like that happens, management steps in. We won't accept it. Nothing that threatens the quality of life of our people is tolerated." Jacques paused for a moment and then added for emphasis, "*Nothing.*"

"If there's a critical client need, we'll re-arrange resources to get it done. But we won't ask people to put in extra hours or threaten their quality of life."

Joe nodded. He got the sense there was a process in place which made re-arranging resources an option. In most companies it was impossible to do that, because everyone was already maxed out. Re-arranging resources was like trying to plug leaks in a dam. By solving one problem you created another. He made a mental note to ask Jacques for more details about what they did instead.

Jacques began walking again and Joe followed, "I've been doing this for over thirty-five years, Joe. One of the biggest lessons I learned early on is when it comes to deciding when people should be at work, it's best to outsource that decision to the person who knows it best."

Joe smiled, "Each individual?"

Jacques nodded, "Exactly. How in the world could I know better than a parent about what schedule would work best in terms of getting their kids to and from school? Or which weeks would be the best to take off for vacation. Why would I ever want to get involved in that?"

"Speaking of vacation time, how much time off do people get who work here?" Joe asked.

"We have a simple vacation policy," Jacques replied. "Take as much as you need." He paused, "We recommend people take the 'normal quantity' and then let them determine what that means."

Joe nodded. It was the first time he'd ever heard of something like that.

"The same goes for sick time," Jacques continued. "One person recently took three months off, during which he was paid the entire time. His wife had been diagnosed with cancer and so we told him to go do what he needed to do and come back when he felt he was able to."

Jacques paused, "You have to look at these things from a longer term perspective, Joe. Could I have been a hard-ass and mandated that the person show up from eight to four every day or they would lose their job? Sure. So then they'd have been here during the day. Then they'd have gone to the hospital from five to eleven-thirty at night. Only with that schedule, they would have been useless at the hospital and useless at work."

He shrugged, "So we tell people to do what they need to do."

"And it works?" Joe asked.

Jacques nodded, "On a lot of levels. First of all, that person is a member of this family. And has been for eighteen years. For almost two decades, he's been there for DLGL. Why would I desert him at the time when he most needs DLGL to be there for him? That would be inhuman.

"Second of all, since people know each other so well here, everyone else in the company sees something like that and knows DLGL stands up for people when they need it. They know if they're ever in that situation, they'll be taken care of too.

"Third of all, when people are in situations like that, and then they come back, they are one hundred percent committed. When they need to step up—they step up.

"Treat people well and they will respond in kind, Joe. That's good for everyone, including the company. I mentioned before, we are in an industry that typically has twenty percent annual turnover. We have zero.

"In large part, that's because of some of the things we've been talking about. What it translates into, is with zero turnover, we are way more efficient and way more effective." He paused for a moment, "And what that translates into, is that we're way more profitable."

Joe nodded. The spirit Jacques had created was similar to what he'd found in all great companies. It was a willingness to treat people right. To trust them to do what was right. And then to reward them for their efforts.

It made common sense. It made good business sense. And yet in so many companies it was rare.

Joe turned to Jacques, "That's a great story you shared about the man who was given the opportunity to be there for his wife. About a month ago I heard almost the opposite story from a friend of mine."

"In what way?"

"She works in one of the big entertainment companies, and one of her peers just went through a similar tough situation. Her husband was diagnosed with cancer and so she was trying to balance being a caregiver and an employee.

"After nine months of working herself to the bone, putting in long days at work and then long hours at the hospital, she was unceremoniously demoted for not doing enough."

Jacques nodded, "How long had she been with the company?"

"Sixteen years."

Jacques shook his head, "I'm sure that did *a lot* for her morale, her well being, her husband's recovery, the morale of the other people in the company...."

He shook his head again, "That's inhuman. And that's the kind of thing that definitely doesn't happen here."

Chapter 15

THE TWO MEN EXITED THE ROOF-TOP AND HEADED down a staircase. In a few minutes they were standing in a hallway area which had an overlook into a gymnasium.

"You have a full gymnasium here?" Joe asked.

Jacques nodded, "We do. This was part of the very original plan. Basketball, volleyball, badminton, floor hockey...."

Joe looked down into the gym. Four people were engaged in a heated badminton match. It was around four o'clock in the afternoon.

"Do you play?" Jacques asked.

Joe shook his head.

"I think it's more popular up here," Jacques replied. "We host tournaments within the company. People sign up for different levels."

Joe looked down at the players. They were really good. "Those must be some of the more advanced players," he said.

Jacques nodded, "Yeah, those are some of the more serious ones."

"What made you build this?" Joe asked and motioned toward the gym.

"Well, like I said, it was always part of the plan. Back when we first started, we all used to play a lot of sports together. It was a pain though. You had to book the gym weeks in advance, then drive to get there, and drive to get back....

"But I saw the bonds it created when we played together. So when we designed the building, I included a gym."

Jacques smiled, "It had more positive effects than I could have ever anticipated. Certainly with the way it has enabled people to bond. Plus it made us famous in our industry. We'd be at a trade show in Vancouver and people would say, 'Hey, are you guys the ones with the gym inside your company?'"

He smiled again, "You have to remember this was more than twenty years ago. No one else was doing this kind of thing. Now you've got Google and other companies who routinely look for ways to bring their people together. But not back then. It made us famous."

"If you want to be interesting, do something interesting," Joe replied.

Jacques nodded, "Exactly. So it helped us get some recognition in the marketplace, which was great. But that was just a little side benefit. The big benefit was what it did for all of us. The truth is, Joe, when people play together, it creates different bonds than when they only work together. No matter how much they enjoy their work.

"I saw that, and so we created tournaments where players would rotate partners every couple of months. That way people really got to know each other. When you play on a team with someone for two months, you get to know them as a human being, not just a co-worker.

"You saw the Vipnasium, up where we met Raquel. We have five people who trained for a year together up there. Then they went and competed in an iron-man competition. Think of the bonds that experience built for those five people. When they reach out to each other for something at work, there's a connection so much deeper than you see among most people in a company. They treat each other better. They know they can rely on each other to a whole other level…."

Jacques shrugged, "I was being interviewed by a journalist one time. After seeing this place and the Vipnasium, and hearing about the hiking trails, bicycles, and the driving range, he asked me if people ever worked.

"He didn't understand. It's all connected. Someone's on the treadmill and comes up with a fantastic idea for our product. Or during their walk in the woods, two team members find a solution to a problem they've been struggling with. It's not like we force those things to happen. They just do. When you do it right, 'life' activities and 'work' activities blend together beautifully. And you end up better in all aspects because of that."

Joe nodded, "So you started with the gymnasium here, and then when you added on, you added the Vipnasium?"

"Uh huh. It was based on the same premise. A lot of people were getting into working out, aerobics and other types of things. They were doing it on their own. We just made it easier for them. The gymnasium stayed the place to play sports. And the Vipnasium became the place to get in shape, train, and work out.

"I've been an athlete since I was a little kid. And I've always been convinced that when I feel good and feel fit, I make better decisions.

I'm smarter. So since I know that's true for me, why not make it available for everyone?

"I've never done the calculation on it, but I know it has paid for itself. People are incredibly fit and healthy. When that's the case, then by default they're not out sick. Which means they're here serving our clients.

"They work out on *their* schedule, in alignment with *their* biorhythm, which means they have higher energy throughout the day. That means higher productivity. They solve things faster, get things done more efficiently, have more energy when they interact with clients and with each other."

He motioned toward the gym, "This place and the Vipnasium are just part of the answer for enabling everyone to be fit and healthy. Twice a day we have someone come through the office with fresh fruits, nuts, and other healthy options. That's all free. If people want junk food, it's in the vending machines in the basement. They have to pay for that. The healthy options are all free."

"It makes sense because it makes sense," Joe said and smiled.

"That it does," Jacques replied.

Just then someone walked into the hallway. It was a man who appeared to be in his late thirties. He was carrying a gym bag and a badminton racquet. It looked like he had just showered off and was heading back to work.

"Hey Jacques. Time to get you out there again," he said. "Demonstrate a few of those moves Denyse Julien taught when she was here."

Jacques smiled and the men shook hands. He introduced him to Joe.

"Do you play?" the man asked Joe.

"Volleyball," Joe replied. "Not badminton. Looks like a great sport though."

"Well, come give it a try if you're interested," the man replied. "We'll teach you. Or come join the volleyball. I'm pretty sure there's a match sometime this week."

The man glanced at his watch, "Sorry guys, I have a call with one of our clients in a few minutes. Joe, nice meeting you. Jacques, are you around later to talk about the new CRM project?"

Jacques nodded, "Sure, just come down to my office. I'll be around."

"He looks like a pretty serious player," Joe commented when the man had walked away.

"Even more so now," Jacques replied. "He mentioned Denyse Julien. For two months we paid her to come in and teach lessons once a week. People got *really* good then."

Joe shook his head, "I'm not familiar with who that is."

"She's a three time olympian and has won thirty-one Canadian National Championships," Jacques replied. He started walking, "Why don't we head this way."

Chapter 16

AFTER SHOWING JOE ONE MORE SECTION OF THE building, and explaining what went on there, Jacques glanced at his watch. It was almost five.

"Joe, we've got two options. We can push on today and cover some more ground. Or we can call it a night and pick things up tomorrow. Now that you've seen a bit of the place, and learned a little about who we are, what do you think you'd like to do as far as getting information for your article?"

Joe looked at Jacques, "I'd like to hang out here for a few days. Maybe even a couple of weeks if you'd be OK with it. You've shared some really interesting things which I know would be great for my project."

"That's good, because we're just getting started," Jacques replied with a smile.

Joe nodded and smiled back, "I get that impression."

"I'll tell you what," Jacques said. "If you're interested in a little light reading tonight, I'll send you off with a gift."

"OK."

Jacques walked over to where his assistant Louise was sitting. "Louise, do you have a moment?"

She turned and smiled, "Sure Jacques. What is it?"

"This is Joe. I mentioned him to you yesterday. He's going to be spending some time with us over the next couple of weeks. I'd like to give him a chance to look through the Big Little Book of Emails tonight. Do you have that handy?"

Joe looked at Louise, "Nice to meet you, Louise."

She smiled, "Nice to meet you too, Joe. Give me just a minute and let me get the book for you."

She reached into a shelf and pulled out a very large, green, three ring binder. It was full of papers. She handed it to Jacques, who in turn handed it to Joe.

"When someone starts at DLGL, we have a very specific goal for them," Jacques said. To comfortably, and with zero stress, enable them to become part of the DLGL team. On their first day, we pair them up with a mentor. They shadow that person every day. Watching, learning, becoming familiar with what happens here.

"There is no expectation they'll come in and 'hit the ground running,' or 'adding value'. This place is a well oiled machine, not a house on fire. They've been hired because as an organization we feel down the line we're going to need another set of hands.

"So in preparation for that, we hired them. At the start, their job is to shadow their mentor, hang out, and really, just to be present. Nothing else. It's the start of a long adventure. In spirit with that, it's important they get familiar with the culture of DLGL."

Jacques indicated toward the binder he'd given Joe, "And that's where the Big Little Book of Emails comes in. When someone starts, we give them that to read."

Joe patted the binder and smiled, "I look forward to going through it. Maybe in the next few days we can talk more about what you just explained. I already have a few questions I'd be curious to know the answers to."

Jacques nodded, "Absolutely." He reached out his hand and Joe took it, "Glad you're here, Joe. We'll see you tomorrow. I'll be in at nine, but show up whenever you want."

Chapter 17

JOE WAS SITTING IN HIS HOTEL ROOM. HE HAD BEEN reading through the Big Little Book of Emails. It was an interesting collection of all kinds of things. Sort of like reading a bunch of small stories.

"Way better than a dry policies and procedures manual," he thought to himself.

Joe was in a good mood. The visit had already been very interesting and it had only just begun.

His phone rang and he glanced at it—Sonia. He hesitated for a minute and then picked it up.

"Greetings from Canada," he said cheerfully.

"Wow, a live person on the other end. This is a nice treat," Sonia said and laughed.

"Yeah, I'm sorry about that. Things have just been a little…," he paused.

She understood why he hadn't taken her calls. Now that she had him on the phone, she wanted to keep the conversation on happier ground.

"What are you doing in Canada?" she asked quickly.

"I'm working on one of my interview pieces. There's a really interesting company here, led by a really interesting guy. I met him today and I'll be staying for a little while. Learning what they do."

Sonia already knew all this. She had spoken with Maggie two days earlier. When Joe had gone silent, she had called Maggie and received an update on what was going on. She didn't like having to hide that from Joe, but he had been on rocky ground lately.

"Anything you can share with me?" she asked.

Joe gave her an overview of what he had seen earlier in the day. Sonia could tell something great had occurred. There was an energy to Joe's voice that hadn't been there in months.

She didn't say much, and instead just let him talk.

"So what's in the Big Little Book of Emails?" she asked, when he got to that part of the story.

"It's very interesting. At first it seems kind of random. I mean the emails cover all kinds of topics. As you read through them though, you realize they are stories which illustrate the culture. And in aggregate, they explain who this company is and the way they do things."

Joe paused, "It's kind of similar to the concept of oral history."

"What's that?" Sonia asked.

"In ancient cultures, people didn't have writing, so they passed on traditions and information orally. They spoke the information. And most of the time, I guess to make it more interesting or easier to understand and remember, the information was conveyed through stories.

"That's kind of what this is. Most companies use a policies and procedures manual to explain the do's and don'ts to a new person. They're usually large, boring books, or very dry pages on the company's intranet. With this, you never know what you're going to get from page to page. Plus, the stories are interesting, so you keep reading.

"In the process, you absorb the same do's and don'ts, and you start to understand and absorb the culture too." Joe grabbed the book, "Here's an example. The subject of the email is Monkeys, Alligators and Dragons."

Sonia laughed, "What?"

"Exactly. Right there it says a lot about the culture. There's an aspect of fun and authenticity. It also inspires you to read the email."

"And what's the content?"

"That one is a de-brief from Jacques, the founder of the company. It's after he attended the ceremony where DLGL was honored for being one of the fifty best managed companies in Canada. They've been on the list fifteen years in a row, by the way.

"He's explaining some of the things he took away from the different speakers at the event."

"Where do the monkeys and alligators come in?" Sonia asked.

"In the stories from the email. It's too much to explain, but here's a few of the take-aways Jacques shares that he found important."

Joe read some of the items.

- Coaching creates Confidence that allows Competence to materialize.
- Know when to apologize, or face cynicism.
- Challenge people to think for themselves. Don't distribute permissions or require approvals.
- Humor is required in business. Per Winnie the Pooh, "This is far too important to be taken seriously."
- Manage yourself so that other's do not have to.

- Performance happens in the right environment.

"In the rest of the email he talks about his experiences at the event and the ways it relates to DLGL," Joe continued. "Like I said, it's the kind of thing where as you read it, without having it beaten over your head, you start to understand what's important for this person and at this company.

"What's interesting, is that some of these emails are really recent and others date back over a decade. Some reflect on events that happened ten years before that. So it really has this sense of tradition to it, which you also see in the content of the emails."

"Are they all on pretty much the same type of topics?" Sonia asked.

"Not even close. They cover all kinds of things. Reasons why they've turned down projects that didn't make sense, dress code suggestions, philosophies on life, impressions of management styles, thank you e-mails after holiday parties.... And they're not all written by Jacques, either. It seems that whenever something gets written which would be a good fit for this book, it gets put in.

"Do you want to hear one?" Joe asked. "This is kind of long, but you'll see what I'm talking about. How the information is so easily transferred."

"Let's hear it," Sonia replied.

Chapter 18

JOE LOOKED AT THE EMAIL AND THEN READ IT TO Sonia.

> From: <j@dlgl.com>
> To: "DLGL" <DLGL@dlgl.com>
> Cc:
> Subject: perfection, imperfections, and selecting between imperfections
>
> We have often said that when one recognizes the fact that nothing will ever be perfect, that person gains a chance of being able to choose the imperfections.
> If somebody is convinced that perfection can be attained and should be pursued at all times, that person will have to live with surprises. Because imperfections will still be there, but they will not have been chosen. They will be unexpectedly forced onto the person who is still focused on perfection at all costs.
> At DLGL, we have certain advantages which are based on the acceptance of imperfections. Like: you are in the work-out center working on your beautiful body at 9:45 am.

The imperfection here is for others. What if somebody needs to talk to you? Well, if your house is on fire, surely your spouse will convince someone to find you in the Vipnasium. If it's someone who needs to know if you can play badminton at five o'clock tonight, it can wait. If it's someone who needs support and you alone have the answer... that person will have to wait. In a perfect organization, that would not happen. But we all know that since nothing is perfect, something else would. Like there would be a procedure for requesting support, a form to fill out, only the system would be down sometimes. Or maybe the folks manning the 800 number would be overworked, so the client would have to take a number and someone would call them back soon.... Probably today....

In order not to have those imperfections, we have selected to have the imperfection that somebody's legitimate call for support, which should be getting immediate attention, might have to wait until you come back from your shower.

And no, preventing you from going to the Vipnasium at 9:45 am is not a solution. It would bring other imperfections which we decided not to have by having a Vipnasium.

This applies to hockey also. It may happen that the three people you need are playing hockey Thursday morning. If indeed you need them, that is an imperfection. But the fact that these support guys play hockey together may be what keeps them smiling for the rest of the day.

Having them not smiling (and yelling at people, including each other, and quitting, and being frustrated on the job) is the imperfection that we decided not to have.

In general, we have absolutely stellar support; ask anybody who has ever been elsewhere.

If somebody feels they need to have a more precise timing handle on support, it is not the responsibility of the folks in support to have the awareness that you cannot live with an imperfection. For example, Paul will be doing an installation at one of our clients next Thursday morning at 7:30 a.m.

So, do like Paul does, and double check with one or more of the support people that they will be available at precisely 7:30 a.m. for help if needed. If you don't know when you may require this absolute support, how the hell is support supposed to know when you will require it?

And no, the perfection of absolute total support at all times will never be available. We are not even trying. We know that would lead to other imperfections, worse than any we have now, and we decided not to have them.

If that is difficult to understand, think of it this way. Imagine if I personally want perfect support. I often work at weird hours. So that would mean I want to be able to call any of you at 10:00 pm on a Sunday night. I need some information, I need an explanation, my computer is down.... Whatever. That would be an imperfection in the lives of everyone at DLGL.

The better imperfection here is that I wait until Monday morning, right? Not that we create a culture where everybody's cell phone must be on 24/7?

A little imagination here will no doubt underline circumstances where your enjoyment of privileges or liberties at DLGL may create an imperfection for somebody else.

And...our systems track time off/non-availability just in case somebody goes nuts in the other direction.

Have a good weekend.

Jacques (Jag) Guénette

Joe finished reading and put down the book. "I know some of that might not make sense because you don't have the details of the company," he said. "But do you see what I mean? Someone who's brand new to the company and reading that, gets an immediate feel for why things exist as they do around the topic of support."

"Even the style in which it's written tells me a lot," Sonia said. "If I knew nothing else but that about this company, I'd already get some strong indications. They tell it like it is, they look at things from a big picture perspective, they value their people...."

She laughed, "I even get the sense they're fun."

"That's what I mean," Joe replied. "You read through these and by default you get this sense of understanding about the culture and what's important."

Chapter 19

"HERE'S ANOTHER ONE," JOE SAID. "IT'S SHORT, AND yet says so much, so quickly. Out of respect for DLGL's privacy, I'll skip the specific names of the clients listed here, but they're right in there so that anyone reading it would know."

From: «Jacques Guénette» <j@dlgl.com>
To: <DLGL@boss.dlgl.com>
Cc:
Subject: Walking the talk

So far this week, we have categorically raised flags with executives (VPs and President) at two of our largest accounts, _____ and _____. Why? Because some of their individuals are not polite and do not show appropriate respect for DLGL employees.

We will pick a fight with anybody, with any consequences, on these issues. That is what is meant when we say that an employee is more important than a client around here. We will not allow abuse of any kind to happen just because the client is issuing the checks.

One case is practically settled, and the other will be before it is over. I guarantee.

Jacques (Jag) Guénette

"Wow!" Sonia said. "*That's* impressive."

"I know," Joe replied. "Imagine you are a new person and you read that. If you have a client who starts pushing you around, you'll know it's OK to let people know. You won't feel intimidated or unsure of what to do. It's right there. It won't be tolerated.

"And whether you'd realize it or not when you read it, on an unconscious level, the fact that it was written over a decade ago and DLGL is still flourishing.... You know it's working."

Joe flipped a couple of pages in the book, "I won't share all of these with you," he said excitedly, "but here's one of the others that really caught my eye. Keep in mind that a lot of what these folks do is about taking data and making sure it's usable and accurate, so that clients can make decisions from it.

"In this message, Jacques takes that to another level by explaining that the data includes the way people within DLGL talk to each other and clients."

From: «Jacques Guénette» <j@dlgl.com>
To: <DLGL@boss.dlgl.com>
Cc:
Subject: Quality of information and Trust

All we do around here is process information. Of all sorts. Its gotta be good.

Good when we get it from clients. We are the experts and must judge when we stop asking questions. When we do, we better have the facts, because that will be the content of our tangible delivery. More data and information based on the information originally gathered.

Good when we exchange it amongst ourselves. To be efficient (which is the absolutely required counterweight to the fact that we are small), we cannot have a highly structured, highly documented, highly controlled modus operandi.

It is all replaced by a presumption of trust, and there must be an actuality of trust, and trust must be justified.

In other words, within DLGL, we need to be able to trust what other people tell us and they need to be able to trust what we tell them. Not sometimes, or most of the time. It has to be all the time.

Trust is the single most valuable asset we can get as a corporation from our clients. And it is the single most valuable asset we can have as individuals from one another.

Don`t screw it up by dealing in little lies, half-truths, omissions, etc. That`s called "being too smart for one`s own good." It catches up no matter how smart someone is. We have had our cases of ultra-smarts…it still caught up eventually.

Quality of information, from any angle.

Jacques (Jag) Guénette

"That's really great," Sonia said.

"Isn't it?" Joe replied. "Such a simple and yet effective way of conveying culture, philosophies, practices…."

Sonia could sense how enthusiastic Joe was and it made her happy. It was an energy she hadn't heard in him in a long time. The type he'd had when they first met.

"Do I sense a future incorporation of some of these concepts into Thomas Derale Enterprises, courtesy of Joe Pogrete?" she asked and laughed.

The words were barely out of her mouth and she was already regretting it. Before the call, she had reminded herself a dozen times. Talk about anything and everything—just don't mention Thomas. The excitement of the conversation had been so authentic though. It just slipped out.

There was silence on the other end of the phone. "Yeah…maybe," Joe replied after a moment.

More silence.

"Joe listen, I was just kidding. I'm sorry I brought up…"

"No, it's OK," Joe said quickly. "It's fine. Really. We're just talking."

It wasn't fine though. She could tell. He was slipping back again toward whatever dark space had been holding him lately.

"Damn it," she said silently to herself.

"Listen, I've got to go," Joe said abruptly. "I want to finish reading this and then head off to bed. Early morning tomorrow."

He was trying to sound cheerful again, but she knew the difference. She wanted to apologize again. To talk him out of that dark space. But she knew there was no point.

"OK," she said with as much energy as she could. "Give me a call in a couple of days and let me know if you've learned to play hockey."

In spite of himself, he smiled, "I will."

Joe hung up. He glanced down at the book, but his energy wasn't into it anymore. Somehow it didn't seem to matter as much now. He closed it and flipped it onto the desk.

Chapter 20

JOE DIDN'T FEEL MUCH BETTER THE NEXT MORNING. After the phone call with Sonia, he had settled into a dark unhappy energy which had been his regular companion for months now.

It troubled him. It reminded him of how he'd felt before Thomas taught him that life could be an ongoing adventure. Not five days of drudgery to be slogged through until the weekend arrived.

It mostly troubled him because he knew it was an insult to Thomas. When your best friend inspires you to live an amazing life, and then they die, you don't turn around and dishonor them by sitting around feeling sad and apathetic. But that's how he felt.

It had been brief, but even so, his half-day at DLGL had connected him to an energy that reminded him of Thomas. Like when the two of them would sit for hours and laugh together as they talked about building things. New companies, crazy products, amazing experiences for the people at Derale Enterprises....

Or when they would co-facilitate Make Me Better sessions. Where they'd get a room of fun, intelligent, passionate people together to collectively push the envelope on what was possible.

For some reason, Joe was pushing back against that positive energy. He knew he should be embracing it. But he found himself holding it at bay.

"Better get it together," he said to himself as he looked in the mirror. "Or this is going to be a *really* short article."

Chapter 21

IT TOOK JUST A MOMENT FROM THE TIME JOE walked into his office, for Jacques to see that something had changed in him from the day before. After thirty plus years of running companies and leading people, Jacques had become very good at picking up on those subtleties.

"Let's get him on some safe ground and get his mind moving," Jacques thought to himself.

"Good morning, Joe. Glad to see you're back," Jacques said with a smile. "I was a little worried the chance of getting you out there with some olympic calibre badminton players might have had you thinking we should finish our conversations over the phone."

Joe focused on returning the smile. Trying to push away the darkness that still hung over him. "Not a chance," he replied. "I'm here."

Jacques got up from his desk, "Perfect. Let's go for a walk, then. There's a part of the building I want to show you. It's one of the keys to our success."

In a few minutes, they were in an area composed of many meeting rooms. They, like the rest of the places in the building, were spacious and had a good feel to them.

"What happens here?" Joe asked.

"In our industry, the common practice is to send the experts out to the client," Jacques replied. "That means for months, sometimes up to a year, people are away from their families, staying in hotel rooms.... And typically, at the client site, they're given whatever space is available." Jacques paused, "Usually the space no one else wants."

Joe nodded, "That's so true. At the start of my career I worked as a strategy consultant. I was amazed at some of the closets and basements we'd be given to work in."

Jacques nodded, "Not exactly the kind of places which inspire great results. Which is why we don't do that. We approach the whole thing differently. Instead of us going to the client for that long stretch of time, we invite the client into our home." He spread his arms and indicated the space around them. "We bring them into a pleasant environment. They have full access to the gym, the workout facility, the mountain bikes..."

"The free fruit," Joe interjected.

Jacques laughed, "All of it. For as long as that part of the project takes, they come here to work and play. And because we bring them *here*, our project isn't competing with other 'To Do List' items, corporate bureaucracy, and all the other distractions they would have if they were at their office.

"This way, the clients are totally focused. Plus it also gives DLGL a chance to go from service provider to friends with the clients. The participants establish a good bond, a deep rapport. Work isn't supposed to be drudgery you try and make it through just to get a paycheck. We demonstrate that here and let the clients experience our version of what it means.

"Down the line, those new friendships lead to a hell of a lot better relationships than if we saw each other as just client and service provider."

"Does it ever just not work out?" Joe asked. "Thinking back on my consulting days, there were some very big egos out there. People wanted things done *their* way, just for the sake of showing off their power."

Jacques nodded, "DLGL walks away from the five percent of crazy clients. If the client doesn't get it, we'll fire them. Sometimes after an initial or second meeting."

Joe smiled, "I bet that creates a little stir for someone with a big ego."

Jacques nodded again, "Oh, yeah. But that's their problem. Not ours."

He indicated the space around them again, "Another big reason we bring the clients to us, is not everyone operates with the same philosophy we do. Not everyone respects their people like we do. This way we keep the control in DLGL's court. We can make sure there's no extra pressure coming down from the client to work long hours or do extra things."

He paused for a moment, "Don't get me wrong, Joe. We're as dedicated towards our clients as we are to our people. This arrangement works for all the reasons we've been talking about. It also works for one more big reason, which is all about the *client*. This method enables us to have the best of the best talent on the job all the time."

"I'm not sure I follow you," Joe said.

"The norm for this industry is that when the sales team sells a new project, it's assigned to whichever consultants happen to be available. Those people may or may not be the best ones for the job. But because they are available, they get the call.

"They may know nothing about the client's industry. They still get the call. They may be brand new and have no experience at all, because the company has twenty percent turnover every year and therefore has to hire a lot of new people. They *still* get the call.

"That's not efficient. It's a big part of the reason why more than sixty percent of these types of projects fail. After many years of effort and tens of millions in investment, they fail."

He shook his head, "Ours don't. We're not interested in someone investing millions of dollars and ending up no better than when they started. So we do things differently.

"When it all takes place here, we can bring in anyone from the DLGL team, at any time. Banking question, we've got people who have done that. Rail, mining, lottery...they've done it. We solve things in one day in a single meeting, which would take months in another setting."

Joe smiled, "And you can still get in some badminton."

Jacques smiled back, "Or ice-hockey if it's Thursday."

Chapter 22

"YOU PLAY ICE-HOCKEY EVERY THURSDAY?"

"This is Canada, Joe. And for as far back as I can remember I've had a hockey stick in my hand every week if not every day."

"You're not telling me you have a hockey rink here?"

Jacques laughed, "No, we rent out a place. One time we booked where the Montreal Canadians play. *That* was an experience. We bought a bunch of tickets for the Canadians game at night, so we got to play on their ice earlier in the day. They even showed a little of our game on the big video screens during the Canadians game."

Jacques smiled, "Most of the time though, we rent out a local hockey arena. Every Thursday morning from seven-thirty to nine." He looked at Joe, "Are you a hockey player?"

Joe shook his head, "Always looked too cold out there," he replied. "And a little rough if you don't know what you're doing."

"Well, maybe we'll inspire you to give it a try," Jacques replied. "The padding keeps you warm." He chuckled, "And it breaks your fall too."

Joe smiled, "I'll keep it in mind."

"We even convinced the restaurant at the rink to open when we're done," Jacques said. "So we play some hockey, grab some breakfast, and head into the office. Everyone gets here by ten or ten-fifteen."

"Does that ever create a problem?"

Jacques nodded, "It could. What it comes down to though is a question of which imperfection is preferable."

Joe smiled, "I remember reading a bit about that in the Big Little Book of Emails."

Jacques nodded again, "I'll give you a deeper explanation. Here's our choices. Choice one is we don't play hockey. That means we've got coverage on Thursdays at nine o'clock, but everyone misses out on the chance to do something they love. Also, no camaraderie is built, no positive energy is created.... That's not a good option.

"Choice two is we book the rink at a time when it's available in the evening. I can tell you from experience that between minor league hockey, and all the rest of what they offer, that would mean we're playing at ten-thirty at night. So a lot of the guys won't be able to play because of family obligations. For those who do play, we get an hour and a half on the ice, grab a shower, and by then it's midnight. Everyone is wired with energy, so we all go out for some drinks.

"By the time everyone gets to bed, it's two in the morning. Then we'll all show up to the office at nine the next day with right around zero energy and a mild hangover. With that option, people are in the office right at nine, and the camaraderie is there, but the rest of it is lousy.

"In comparison, choice three, which is what we do now, starts looking really good. No one needs to miss out because of family obligations. It's a great start to the morning. The positive energy it creates flows throughout the day. We get some extra time on the ice because no one else is interested in playing in the morning. Everyone gets breakfast. The camaraderie is there. And the only issue is, for that first hour every Thursday morning, there's a chance the person whose expertise is needed, isn't available."

Jacques nodded, "And it did happen. *Once*. One day out of fifty two weeks times thirty years, we had an issue where all three people who could have solved the problem, were playing hockey. But that is a preferable imperfection compared to the imperfections choices one and two would create."

Jacques shrugged, "I love detail, Joe. Build it right, build it beautifully, make every line, every component the right one.... Yet I also realize one of the biggest mistakes people make when they build, is they build systems with the goal of perfection, instead of the goal of excellence.

"All life has imperfections. There's no way around that. So better to pick the imperfections you prefer, so you can manage them on *your* terms, than to have the unexpected imperfections show up unexpectedly."

Chapter 23

JOE WAS SITTING IN JACQUES' OFFICE. HIS TIME AT DLGL was passing quickly. It was his fourth day there.

Jacques was finishing up a phone call and as he did, Joe was reflecting on one of their conversations. Jacques had been explaining his view on attention to detail. How it didn't mean waiting until things were perfect before he would start. Instead it meant continuing to grow and perfect and enhance what he was working on, so it continually got better.

It reminded Joe of the ascending life curve. A concept Thomas had taught him and Joe had in turn taught many others. As Joe thought about that, his mind brought back many memories. In particular, ones from Thomas' last television interview before he died.

Joe desperately tried to push the memories from his mind. He knew what would accompany them. But the more he tried to push them away, the stronger they became. And with them, came the inexplicable flood of emotions, the darkness, and the feelings of depression.

"Joe?"

"Joe?"

Joe shook his head and came out of the daze he had been in. For a moment he wasn't sure where he was. Then he gathered himself. "Hey, Jacques. Sorry."

"You OK? You looked like you were deep in thought."

"Oh, I…I just had a memory come back to me. Something I haven't thought about in a while."

Jacques hesitated. Over the last five days, he had noticed that at random times, Joe would sort of disappear mentally for a few minutes. When he came back, he always had a sadness in his face and it took him a while to re-engage. Jacques decided this was the time to start digging a little bit.

"Joe, we've been talking an awful lot about DLGL these last days. Let's turn things around for a few minutes. Tell me about where you're at—Derale Enterprises. What's it like there?"

Joe sat for a moment, getting himself together. "Where to start," he wondered.

"The center around which we revolve is a concept called the Big Five for Life," he began. "It's a simple thing, and yet I can tell you from experience, the power that comes from it is astounding."

"What is it?" Jacques asked.

"Every day we all have choices. How we spend our time, where we spend our money, what we allocate our energy to, the things we think about…. Most people make those choices in a reactionary mode. Someone in their life dictates, entices, or pushes, and the person responds.

"But living and working that way doesn't result in a whole lot of great moments. You just end up going wherever everyone else wanted you to go in life. Just by their nature, some people find their way out of that. They make a conscious decision to move their life in the direction *they* want it to go.

"And that's really the essence of what the Big Five for Life is. It's asking yourself what are the five things you most want to do, see, or experience during your life. Then aligning all your time, energy, money, thoughts, and other resources to make that happen."

Jacques nodded, "Interesting."

"It is. And so logical when you hear it. Yet for most people, when they learn about it, it's the first time they realize *they* get to set the destination for their life. *They* are in control of their own existence.

"Life isn't merely a response to whatever emails, news reports, texts, parent advice, or any of a thousand other sources of input are telling you what to do. Life is about choosing what *you* want to do.

"Within the culture at Derale Enterprises, the Big Five for Life is a part of everything. Whether someone is looking to try a new role, reward their team members, distribute new opportunities...it always goes back to—what is on that person's Big Five for Life list?

"We have a mentoring program for new people. Very similar to what you do here. And one of the first conversations between the mentor and mentee is they share their Big Five for Life with each other.

"When we interview people who are interested in working for us, the Big Five for Life is a very significant part of those discussions. If the candidate doesn't understand the essence of it, or the concept isn't a good fit for them, they won't be a good fit for our organization. If their Big Five for Life aren't in alignment with the job they'd be doing, that won't be a good fit either."

Joe smiled, "Do you remember when you were talking about the sports programs you have here? How when people play together, the dynamic and the relationship between them changes?"

Jacques nodded.

"It's the same with the Big Five for Life." Joe smiled again, "I love traveling. That's one of *my* Big Five for Life. And one of my favorite areas of the world is Southeast Asia. In that part of the world, there is this beautiful expression. It's called 'namaste.' The essence of what that word means, is—'I see you.' Not that I physically see you, but that I really *see* you. I see the essence and the energy, and the spirit of you.

"In my mind, when your people play sports together, that's what's happening. People *see* each other. No longer is someone 'Tony from support.' They become real, human, alive.... They laugh together, share experiences, play, bond, celebrate, try....

"The same thing happens in our companies. Since we look at each other through the lens of each other's Big Five for Life, we constantly *see* each other. In everything we do, talk about, the decisions we make…there is that connection to what matters most to us in life."

Joe shrugged, "I've learned that most people want to have meaning in their life. Meaningful conversations, meaningful minutes…. It's not the desire that's missing. What's missing is the path to make 'meaning' a significant part of their everyday reality.

"Knowing, aligning their resources around, and then living their Big Five for Life…. That has proven to be a really effective path for our people to have that meaning."

Jacques was listening to Joe, and also watching him intently. This was the most animated he'd seen him in all their days together. He was talking from the heart. Jacques sensed it was time to push him a little more.

"How did you discover Derale Enterprises, Joe?"

Chapter 24

JOE PAUSED. HIS MIND WAS SEARCHING. HE KNEW the answer to Jacques' question, but each time his mind went to that memory, it tried to escape. He could only hold it for a few seconds and then there was a silence, a numbness which would start to overtake him.

Joe looked at Jacques. Then he looked away. His mind still racing to the memory and then trying to escape it. "I met the founder, Thomas Derale, while waiting for a train one morning," he finally said.

He looked down. His eyes were beginning to water. He quickly blinked and looked away, trying to hide the emotion.

Jacques saw all of this. He'd witnessed a lot in thirty plus years of leading people. He'd had a lot of conversations where it was just him and another person, sitting in the same two seats as he and Joe were sitting in now. Wedding announcements, babies being born, kids getting into college…. And conversations on sad topics too. Spouses being diagnosed with an illness, the death of parents.

"On a train?" Jacques interjected, helping Joe deal with the emotions he was feeling. "Sounds like there's a good story there."

Joe looked up at Jacques. And for the first time in a long time, when his mind went back to the memory of meeting Thomas, he didn't try to push it away.

Joe nodded, "Uh-huh. On a cold winter morning while waiting for a train. We were complete strangers. He asked me if it was a good 'museum day morning.' I had no idea what that meant at the time. Had no idea I'd end up learning about the Big Five for Life, or working with Thomas...." Joe shook his head, "None of it."

"What's the significance of 'museum day?'" Jacques asked.

Joe looked off into a corner of the room. His mind raced to another memory. This time of wheeling Thomas through his museum, shortly before he died. To Joe's surprise, he didn't immediately try and push away that memory either.

Joe shifted his gaze back to Jacques. He shook his head a little, bringing himself back to the present. "It's another part of what Thomas created in his companies. Another way of helping all of us look at what we do each day from a different perspective.

"He explained it to me the second time I met him. It was on the train, a week after he'd first spoken to me. The concept is simple, just like the Big Five for Life. Just as profound too."

Joe's mind flashed once again to the night he'd walked with Thomas through the museum of his life. He could see the images, the exhibits, the plaque with Thomas' final message to everyone who worked with him....

"Imagine if every day of our life was cataloged," Joe began. "The way we felt, the people we saw, how we spent our time. And at the end of our life, a museum was built. It was built to show exactly how we lived our life. If eighty percent of our time was at a job we didn't like, then eighty percent of our museum would be dedicated to showing us unhappily spending our time at that job we didn't like.

"If we were friendly with ninety percent of the people we interacted with, it would show that. But if we were angry and upset or yelled at ninety percent of the people we interacted with, it would show that.

"If we loved the outdoors, or spending time with our kids, or celebrating life with our significant other, but only spent two percent of our life fueling those loves, then no matter how much we wished it to be different, only two percent of our museum would be dedicated to that.

"Imagine what it would be like to walk that museum toward the end of our life. How would we feel? How would we feel knowing that for the rest of eternity, that museum would be how we were remembered? Every person who walked it would know us exactly as we truly were. Our legacy would be based not on how we dreamed of living...but how we lived.

"Now imagine if heaven, or the afterlife, or however we individually think this all works, actually consists of us being the tour guide for our own museum—for all of eternity."

Joe had shared the museum day concept countless times from the stage, using the same words he had just spoken. As he was saying them to Jacques, his mind was racing to so many different memories. Different times when he'd been at events with Thomas, when they'd shared the stage together, or laughed in Make Me Better sessions....

"That *is* a powerful concept," Jacques said quietly.

Joe nodded.

"You miss Thomas, don't you?" Jacques asked.

Joe's eyes watered again. He blinked quickly and looked away.

Both men sat in silence for a few minutes.

"He was my best friend," Joe finally said. "What he taught me changed my life forever. I wouldn't have the life I do, wouldn't *view* life the way I do, if it wasn't for him."

Joe shook his head, "A little over a year ago we did an event together at one of our company gatherings. When it was done, we shook hands, said we'd see each other soon, and then I left on a trip. A couple of months later, Maggie emailed me and told me Thomas was sick. Then a few months later…he was gone. Just like that."

Joe's eyes filled with tears. He blinked and looked away again.

"He was only fifty-five years old," he finally said. He shook his head a little, "I don't know why, but…" Joe shook his head again, "but I can't get past it somehow. I try. I really do. I speak at events, I give interviews. All the things that used to be so great…."

Jacques sat silently. Listening. Watching.

Joe looked up at the corner of the room again, "When I first learned Thomas was dying, I didn't believe it. He was 'life' personified. He connected with people and made them feel special. In meetings he was always the one who brought light and energy into the situation. No matter how challenging it was, he would find some ridiculous, funny perspective, or some truly inspired way of looking at it.

"He and Maggie and I would travel together and they had this incredible relationship. The kind of stuff you see in the movies, where it almost seems too good to be real. They had that."

Joe paused, "When I learned he was dying, I stayed with Thomas and Maggie. Trying to help out where I could. Every morning I'd come downstairs expecting him to be fine. That it was all just a horrible dream I'd had. But it wasn't a dream."

Joe looked at Jacques, "There was this huge event for him. His fellow travelers from across his life—friends, people he worked with, clients, customers.... They'd worked tirelessly once it was clear he was dying and had built this incredible museum of his life...."

Joe looked away again, the emotions flooding back to him. Despite his efforts to blink them away, tears began to flow down his cheeks. "When the celebration was over, he and I went through the museum together. His illness was so advanced by then, he couldn't walk anymore and was in a wheelchair. I rolled him through each piece of his museum. I watched him say goodbye."

Joe wiped away the tears, "That's when it really hit me. That's when I realized my best friend was really dying."

He shook his head, "A few days later he was gone."

Joe sat silently for a few moments.

"And no matter how much I try to pretend everything is OK, and that *I'm* OK.... No matter how much I try to settle back into life…" He shook his head, "It just doesn't seem the same. Things just don't feel meaningful anymore."

Chapter 25

JOE DIDN'T SLEEP MUCH THAT NIGHT. AFTER THEIR conversation about Thomas, he and Jacques decided to call it a day. Jacques told him to take a break and arrive in the afternoon the next day.

Joe had returned to his hotel and then gone for a long walk. Hours later he was back at his hotel, but he felt as empty as when he'd left Jacques' office.

It was like a physical weight was laying on his chest. And no matter what he did, he couldn't get rid of it.

The next morning, the weight was still there. It was still there at noon too. Joe thought about calling Jacques and telling him he was sorry, but he couldn't finish the interview. Nothing about that felt right either though.

When he arrived at the DLGL offices in the early afternoon, Joe was greeted by DLGL's Director of First Impressions. She smiled and said hello. Joe smiled back, but he felt empty. The smile felt empty.

Jacques had been watching Joe walk from the parking lot up to the entrance to DLGL. "Push a little more, or back off?" he asked himself. He could see Joe hadn't slept. There were bags under his eyes even though it was now afternoon.

When Joe knocked at the door to his office, Jacques took one more look at him and made his decision. "Good afternoon, Joe," he said with a smile. "Come on in."

Joe entered the office and took a seat.

The two men sat in silence for a few moments. Then Jacques leaned forward in his chair. "Yesterday you told me part of your story, Joe. I appreciate that. It takes a great deal of courage for one human being to open up to another. Especially to someone they haven't known for a long time."

Jacques paused and let that sink in. "Today I'd like to tell *you* a story. It's about DLGL, so I think you'll find it useful for your article. And it's about friendship. And I think you'll find that useful for your life right now."

Joe nodded, unsure of what to say.

"Let's take a walk," Jacques said.

He got up and led Joe through the DLGL offices. After a few minutes, they entered a long, beautiful hallway that Joe hadn't been in before. One side of it had large windows which opened to the outdoors. There were beautiful views of the forest which bordered the company. On the other side of the hallway was a long wall filled with pictures.

Jacques stopped at one of the first ones. It was a picture of a house overlooking a river. Two men were standing in front of it.

"Is that you?" Joe asked.

"A lot younger back then," Jacques said with a smile. "That's a picture of the first DLGL office."

"A house?"

Jacques nodded, "We started there. Then when we outgrew that, we bought the house next door and worked out of both of them.

When we outgrew that, we bought the next one over and worked out of all three."

He smiled, "Everyone would leave their keys in the ignition, so when you had to go somewhere you could move whoever's car might be in your way."

Joe was looking at the different pictures of the houses and the people in front of them. "You moved from there to here?"

"Eventually, yes. Then we almost lost everything and had to start all over again." He shrugged, "We came as close as you can to going under. But we didn't. And now here we are, twenty years later, going strong."

Joe looked at the pictures again. "Who is this with you in front of the house?"

"That's Claude Lalonde. He and I were the crazy ones who founded DLGL."

"It's his picture that's in your office, isn't it?" Joe asked. "The portrait on the wall?"

Jacques nodded. Then he pointed to the photograph Joe had been looking at, "Claude and I met about ten years before that picture was taken. We first got to know each other when I invested in a company and he was the guy in charge of systems. Eventually I joined the company as CFO and he made the decision to invest some money and take an ownership position too. So initially we were connected by that."

Jacques smiled, "It was a good connection. We saw things the same way most of the time in business matters. We made decisions at the same speed, which is very important. And we liked and respected each other too. We met through the business, but we became friends because we genuinely got along well."

"When that company closed, we stayed connected. He would show up at my house every morning and we'd go running." Jacques laughed, "Then I came up with a crazy idea for a new company, and we put the collective one thousand five hundred dollars we both had into it." He laughed again, "Unfortunately that one didn't go very far.

"Then one day along came the fourth generation computer programming languages. Claude was really excited about that. He had spent years building deep expertise in payroll systems for large employers. He felt that with the fourth generation languages, at last we had the tools to write the systems people needed. He had envisioned the systems and now saw ways to make them real.

"He knew it was big, and he came to me and said let's do it. That's how DLGL got started. He began working on the technology and I started mapping out the business. At the time, I had developed a consultancy in interim management. And I had a wife and three kids to take care of. So I kept the consultancy going as a safety net in case we proved to ourselves we were nuts. That meant my contributions would come in the evenings and on the weekends."

Joe nodded, "Clearly you weren't nuts."

Jacques shook his head a little, "No. Claude saw it right." He chuckled, "Although it was far from a smooth ride for us to get from that start to what you see today."

Joe moved down the wall a little. There was a contract in a frame, "Your first client?"

Jacques nodded, "When we started, we began with who we knew and who knew us from all our previous work. That was a good start. We didn't have a big team or a huge brand, but our expertise in payroll systems was so concentrated that our size became irrelevant.

"When we were fourteen people, we were in a meeting with NORTEL, which was a huge company back then. Probably thirty thousand people or more. We were sitting with a bunch of their senior people and the CFO said, 'What is NORTEL doing dealing with a fourteen person corporation along a river in Montreal?'"

Jacques smiled, "Little did he know it was fourteen people working out of a house."

Joe laughed, "What did you tell him?"

"I told him the truth. That we were the largest for the task at hand and we had the deepest pool of expertise too. That was enough. They bought it. The team grew to twenty-two or twenty-three while we were serving them."

Joe moved even farther down the wall. There was a picture of an airplane with a large, red maple leaf and the words Air Canada written on it. "Another client?" he asked.

"Yes, and a defining moment in the company's history," Jacques replied.

Chapter 26

JACQUES MOTIONED TO THE PICTURE OF THE airplane, "Up to that point, getting customers wasn't really driven by a particular strategy. We were doing a good job, people were talking, and it just happened.

"With Air Canada, they published an RFP. At that point, DLGL had been around for about thirteen years and had a good reputation. So after answering the RFP, we got the job. Our proposal back then was we know payroll and pensions and computers. Tell us what you need and we'll develop it. Whatever programming language you want, we'll do it."

Jacques shrugged, "And Air Canada was the last client where we did it like that."

Joe nodded, "What happened?"

"After we'd been working with them for about eighteen months, we got a letter saying they were canceling the project. They were very apologetic. It had nothing to do with us. They were very happy with all we'd done and offered to issue letters of recommendation to that effect. But budgets had tightened, their business was down, and they couldn't fund the project anymore."

Jacques shrugged, "They represented almost 100% of our income stream. And just like that…they were gone."

Joe retraced his steps down the wall a bit, still looking at the pictures and tracking the events through the images. "You were in this building already by then, weren't you?" he asked, pointing to one of the pictures

"Barely," Jacques said. "We'd only been here eight months when we got the letter."

"Wow."

"Wow indeed. After thirteen years, we were at a critical juncture in the life of the company. Everything we'd built was poised to go away."

Jacques moved down the wall and pointed at a picture of a wrought iron bench, with wood slats. It was sitting on a bluff, surrounded by large trees and overlooking a river.

"In addition to working in the two houses, Claude and I and our families each lived in one of those houses. And in between them was this bench. The one you see in this picture. We'd go there almost every night to talk. State of the union for the business, whatever challenges we were dealing with, state of the union for our lives….

"After we got the notice from Air Canada, we had a lengthy discussion on that bench. Because we had some big decisions to make. We could have folded shop, sold the building and retired. If not forever, at least for a really long time. The business had been very profitable and we'd been smart about putting money away.

"The big capital investment we'd made was the building and we knew we could sell that if we needed to."

"Did you consider that?" Joe asked. "Folding up shop and retiring?"

Jacques laughed, "Sort of."

"What do you mean?"

"There's lots of things which make people good business partners. And good friends too. One of them is a similar speed in which you make decisions. When your decision making is synchronized, you can work together for a long time. If not, it gets real painful, real fast. Claude and I had that similar speed.

"For the decision about the company, we sat on the bench and talked about our options. Then Claude, in his typical Claude way, asked some funny philosophical question like—'And what the fuck are we going to do with all our time if we retire?'"

"I'd give him an answer and he'd respond with—'And then what? And then what?'

"And we realized we liked what we were doing. For most people, they can't wait to retire so they can go do what they like. Well, we were already doing that."

Jacques laughed, "Claude kept coming up with these arguments about what an 'opportunity' our situation was. No clients. What an opportunity! A great time to look forward, not back! Now we take all we learned and really do it the *right* way."

"Which meant?" Joe asked.

"Which meant moving from a service company where we would build whatever anyone wanted, to a product company. We would create an incredible product, which we knew from all our expertise, companies needed and wanted. A beautiful system which would be around for decades."

Jacques smiled, "Claude asked me if we could pull it off financially? I asked him how long it would take to create a system like he was envisioning. In typical Claude fashion, he said, 'three to four months.' So I said, how about in eight to nine months? 'Oh yeah, definitely,' he replied."

Joe smiled, "How long did it take?"

"More than a year."

Jacques smiled and looked away, remembering. "During that meeting on the bench, I told him look, let's say we make our decision to move forward with this idea. We have the money that's in the company. We have the building. And we have our personal assets.

"There will come a point where if things don't turn out well, we will have lost all our cash reserves. At that point, we will be left with the building and our personal assets. Then there will come another point where we've burned through the equity in the building, and that's gone. Then a final point where we'll lose our houses, our pension funds, and everything else. We should agree to meet at each of these critical checkpoints and ask ourselves again if we are doing the right thing."

Jacques smiled, "And then it was done. The decision was made. We sat on the bench and talked a few things over. We laughed. And that was that."

"You put a lot at risk," Joe said. "You must have really trusted him."

Jacques nodded, "If you were going to go to war with someone, that was the guy you wanted with you. You knew no matter what, he had your back. And you had his."

Chapter 27

JOE CONTINUED DOWN THE HALLWAY AND LOOKED at the next image. It was a check from the provincial government.

"Were they your first client for the new software?"

Jacques shook his head, "They were our lifeline when we were about to drown.

"The day after Claude and I made the decision to move forward, we sat down with our three most key people. We asked them what the optimal group would be to conserve capital and deliver the system Claude was imagining. At that time, we had thirty-five people.

"We also knew we'd need different skill sets for what we were going to become. So that was part of the discussion too. When all the talking was done, the decision was to scale back to twenty-one people. Which meant fourteen were going to lose their jobs."

"Not a fun moment, I'm sure," Joe said.

Jacques shook his head. "Nope. Claude took the twenty-one who were staying and I took the fourteen who were being let go. We told everyone all at once what was going on and what we had decided. It wasn't a question of commitment from them. It was the only option if we were going to have a future. I told my group that if we could get things going quickly, and there was a good fit for them, we'd try and bring them back."

Jacques shook his head again, "The tough part was the one-on-ones with each person after the group meeting. There was nothing to say which hadn't been said as a group. And yet you want to somehow try and let them know you wish it were different."

He looked at Joe, "When all the one-on-ones were done, I sat for a while in my office. Around seven o'clock, someone came in and said I should get going, that everyone was at the pub. Everyone? Yeah, everyone.

"And they were. All the ones who were staying. All the ones who had just lost their jobs. And when I walked in and saw them all together, that's when it hit me the hardest. There was so much cohesion in that group. These people meant so much to each other."

Jacques paused and Joe could see that the emotion was still there, even after all those years.

"When I walked in and saw everyone together, I just thought—what have we done?" Jacques said.

He shook his head, "We were at the bar until five in the morning. Everyone drunk and crying. Then laughing and crying again."

"Did any of them ever get hired back?"

"Some. Others had moved on to other things by the time we were hiring again. Or in some cases, the skills we needed were different from what they had."

Jacques looked at the pictures on the wall, "If you look hard enough, Joe, and are willing to be really honest with yourself, those are the type of situations where you learn some of your biggest lessons. I remember in one of our first meetings after that, I drew a temple with one leg. That's what our situation had been with Air

Canada. Then I drew another temple with lots of legs. That's where we were going.

"Our security would be in two aspects. First, we'd make sure we were diversified with our client base. Second, we'd put in place things like recurring revenue streams which was something we didn't have before. The experience challenged us to look at our model in all aspects.

"Before that, we'd create a product, the client would use it for a few years and then junk it. Not this. We wanted to be with our clients for *decades*."

Jacques pointed to a picture of a pillar and a temple on the wall. "This is here to remind us of that day and what we learned. It's famous in the company now. People still refer to it. The pillar and the temple."

"Why is this happening to me?" Joe said.

Jacques looked at him.

"A piece of our culture," Joe added. "Powerful in business. Powerful in life too. When things go in a different direction than we want, it's tempting to drop into the victim mentality—'Why is this happening to *me*?'

"The same words, but said with a different intonation, change the answers you get when you ask the question. We challenge each other, and ourselves, to ask—Hmmm, w*hy* is *this* happening to me?

"That subtle shift changes the whole focus from one of a victim, to a seeker. What can I learn? What insight can I gain?"

Jacques nodded, "I like that. And it's true. What we experienced with Air Canada enabled us to be the company we are now. Our pillars are strong and so are our financial resources. Our product is incredible. Our clients have been with us for long periods…." He nodded, "We looked at what could have been the end and turned it into the start."

Joe looked again at the check on the wall from the provincial government. "You said this was your lifeline that kept you from drowning. How close did you come to going under with the new business?"

"Well, do you remember those big check points I mentioned earlier?"

Joe nodded.

"We went through all of them. We came within two weeks of completely running out of money."

Chapter 28

JACQUES LOOKED AT JOE, "AT THE FIRST CHECK point, we had gone through all the cash we'd put away. Then we mortgaged the building to the hilt. Sold all the assets. Did what could be done with the pension fund."

Jacques looked down for a few moments, then looked at Joe again, "My assistant, Louise, came in one day during that period. She had gone home and talked with her husband. She offered to lend us five thousand dollars. It was a great deal of money for them, and they offered to lend it to us to help keep things going."

Jacques' eyes watered as he remembered the event. He looked away.

Joe nodded, letting the significance of the story sink in. "That's amazing," he replied after a few moments. "What did you tell her?"

Jacques paused and shook his head, "I cried. I don't know. The stress level was extremely high I guess. And she had to know there was a real risk the money would never be recovered. The five thousand dollars wasn't going to make the difference, but she wanted to do *something*. She *and* her husband. And those funds to them was a significant chunk of money."

He looked up at Joe, "To this day it's something I'm grateful for. The level of confidence that she had in us and the willingness to do whatever she could."

"She still here, isn't she?" Joe said. "She's the Louise I met earlier."

Jacques nodded, "Oh yeah." He smiled, "My boss."

"So you were two weeks away from running out of capital. And then this check showed up?"

Jacques nodded, "We had made a claim for an R&D expense almost a year earlier. It was a refund of income taxes we had paid. And completely out of the blue, the check came in at that moment."

"How long did that carry you for?"

"It was a fair chunk of change. About five months. Right about to the time when we were getting close to running out again."

Joe shook his head, "Those were such big decisions. You're a Dad, a husband. Your personal assets are all going away. What made you keep going?"

Jacques nodded, "We had confidence in what we were doing. The future was in that direction. We knew it. Product based. We knew we had the competencies to get it done, because we had great people.

"Also, what we were creating was a beautiful product. It still is, now in its eighth generation." He shook his head a little, "That's what we did. Who we were. We built systems. And this was a *heck* of a system. There was nothing like it. That was more important than the money."

He shrugged, "And on top of that, you've got twenty-one people who have accepted this challenge with you. And they go home and out with friends, and people are saying, 'Why don't you get out now before everyone else is out there looking for a job too.' But they stuck to it. They took the proposal we offered and they lived by it.

"They didn't leave the ship. So there was no way on earth Claude and I were going to leave the ship before anyone else. That was darn sure. These people who decided to stick with it were taking a personal gamble too. They stuck to their word and we were going to stick to ours.

"Claude was a very proud man and so am I. Show me a proud man and I'll show you a man you can trust. They trusted us and we weren't going to stop until we dropped dead."

Joe nodded, "Luckily it didn't come to that."

Jacques shook his head, "No. We got lucky again. Unbelievably lucky."

Chapter 29

JACQUES MOVED DOWN THE WALL TO A PICTURE OF people celebrating.

"Back in those days," he began, "IBM was in the manufacturing business. They had a company they spun off, called Celestica. They're a huge manufacturer of components. And the spinoff had to be done by December 31st.

"Everything done prior to that day was IBM's expense. Anything after that, the spinoff company had to pay for on their own. So they went out and bought everything they thought they would need. Including systems. And one of those systems was ours—VIP.

"At that point, VIP was fresh out of the oven. As a matter of fact, it was still really in the oven. A lot of vaporware."

Jacques laughed, "Of all the people on earth to buy vaporware—IBM. Had it not been so dramatic of circumstances for us, it would have been funny."

He smiled, "When we signed that deal it was a hell of a Christmas, I'll tell you that. And a hell of a few months after too. The phone would ring in January and the guys would walk into my office and say, 'Hey, the client just called. They want a list of reports.'

"Oh yeah, reports. We need reports. OK, what did we have at Air Canada and see which ones we are going to re-do."

Jacques smiled again, "There was an enthusiasm and an energy and a mode of creation that was really something great. And in some respects it probably worked out better that Celestica got us at the stage we were at. We built exactly what they needed and then expanded from there."

He smiled, "Claude used to have this expression—'Exciting times.' Whenever we'd have something like this, where you could feel the energy and the enthusiasm.... You could see this incredible future and almost couldn't wait to be a part of it all.... 'Exciting times', he would say. 'Exciting times.'

"In the life of DLGL, those truly were exciting times."

Chapter 30

JOE WALKED A LITTLE FARTHER DOWN THE HALLWAY, looking at the pictures. Something was nagging at him. At first he couldn't figure it out. Then all of a sudden, it hit him. As he looked at the images from company events, funny moments with client teams, other gatherings, there came a point where Claude was no longer in the pictures.

Joe hesitated. His heart began to beat faster. He wanted to ask. Yet at the same time, he didn't want to know the answer. Eventually he turned to Jacques, "What happened to Claude?" he asked quietly.

Jacques nodded. Then he smiled a little. It was a smile of reflection. There was a fondness in it. A hint of sadness too. "Let's go downstairs," he said.

He led Joe to a stairwell which wound down a level. They were in a part of the building Joe hadn't been to before. Jacques hadn't purposely kept Joe away from it. But his instincts had told him there would be a specific time to bring Joe here. This was the time.

They turned a corner and Jacques opened a door and let Joe walk in. They entered into what felt like a sports bar. There was wood paneling on the lower half of the walls, sports memorabilia hanging everywhere, restaurant style tables available for sitting....

Joe looked to his left. There was even a real bar. Fully stocked from the looks of it. And overhanging the bar, a blue neon sign all lit up—"Bistro chez Claude."

He looked to his right. The walls were full of pictures. They were funny. Memorable. People being silly and having a great time.

"The people of DLGL at their most ridiculous," Jacques said. "A piece of our culture every bit as important as anything else."

Farther into the room along the same wall was a large trophy full of inscriptions.

"Winners of the badminton tournaments," Jacques said. "They get their name immortalized there."

Joe smiled. "And that," he asked and motioned toward the corner where there were about thirty broken badminton racquets and a broken hockey stick all jammed into a small trash can.

Jacques smiled too, "Not all the matches go as well as players would like. And sometimes they get a little upset with themselves. The racquets pay the price."

"Hockey stick too, I guess," Joe added.

"We could probably put a couple dozen more of those in there to be honest," Jacques added.

Joe walked farther into the room. There were pictures of hockey players. They were wearing jerseys with V.I.P. on them. Joe saw that Jacques was in the pictures. "Is this all the people who play hockey here in the company?"

Jacques nodded.

"I like the jerseys," Joe said.

"If it's worth doing, do it right," Jacques replied.

"You sponsor a racing team?" Joe asked and pointed at a picture of a race car with 'DLGL' on the side.

"We do. The thing I like about racing is that it's like life but in fast forward. You do your work, you prepare, all the players gather in Daytona together, and you get your report card right there. How did we do? Then you go away, you prepare again, and two weeks later in Houston you get another report card.

"Life is pretty much the same way. You prepare, you do, you get a report. Those who do the right things end up winning. They live a great life. As you described it, they create an amazing museum for themselves.

"Those who never get in the race, never adjust, never grow or adapt, they just sort of disappear. They don't really win the game of life."

Joe looked closer at one of the pictures of the race car. The car was being worked on by the pit crew. It looked like Jacques was the driver. "Is that just for the picture, or do you really drive?"

Jacques nodded, "I'm one of the drivers."

Joe turned and surveyed the whole room. "Is this really a bar?"

"Bistro chez Claude," Jacques replied.

"And people can come down here anytime?" Joe asked.

Jacques nodded. "Sure. The bar is stocked. It's for the people here at DLGL."

"What was your motivation for creating this?" Joe asked.

"It's a tribute to Claude. A place where people can go and relax after work if they want, without having to actually go out somewhere. Someplace fun. It's open all the time. Everyone has access.

"It's funny," he continued. "Most companies have an executive floor. There's usually free food and a bar somewhere up there. But it's only for the executives, not for the rest of the employees. As if the executives can be trusted to not get drunk during the day, or drink the company's expensive alcohol, but not everyone else."

Jacques paused, then motioned toward a table. "Let's grab a seat and talk for a minute, Joe."

Chapter 31

THE TWO MEN SAT IN SILENCE FOR A FEW MOMENTS. Joe was thinking about the images on the wall upstairs. How Claude had stopped being in the pictures.

Finally, Joe broke the quiet, "Claude died didn't he?"

Jacques nodded slowly.

Joe looked away, his eyes filling with tears. He was so tired of that response. He wished it would go away, but it was like an automatic reaction whenever he was somehow connected with Thomas' death.

Joe blinked to clear the tears. Then he turned back toward Jacques. "What happened?" he asked quietly.

Jacques leaned back in his seat, remembering. "In Claude's case, it stretched out over a pretty long period of time. He gave me a call one day and said we should go to lunch. I didn't think anything of it, but at lunch he told me he'd been feeling like something was wrong. So he'd gone in for an exam. They'd done some tests and it looked like something *was* wrong, but they didn't know what. So they were going to send him for even more tests."

Jacques sighed, "So then we waited. Hoping it would be nothing. When the results eventually came back, they knew it was something bad. They didn't know exactly what. So back Claude went for another round of tests. Little by little, it started to sink in that something pretty serious was wrong.

"Eventually they came back and told him they'd figured it out. It was colon cancer. He did a surgery. We hoped that would take care of it. But it didn't. And at that point, Claude decided he wasn't going to try anything fancy. No chemo, no radiation. He would get a certain level of treatment and after that, if it didn't work, he would refuse anything more."

Joe nodded, "What did you think about that?"

"I knew the subject wasn't worth discussing a whole lot. He had a picture in his head of what he would do depending on the situation. There wasn't much I could say to change his mind."

Jacques shrugged, "I tried to give him examples. When they did his surgery they learned his colon was perforated. It was leaking badly. The doctors told him he was really lucky. That they had just got in some new piece of equipment a day earlier which allowed them to sew things together in a much tighter fashion. It would prevent the need for him to carry around one of those bags to clean his kidneys.

"So I told Claude that somebody had probably been using that type of machine for years somewhere else. So maybe there'd be something else out there if we went and looked." Jacques shook his head, "But he said he wasn't going to get into that kind of battle. No drama.

"He had a close friend who was a doctor who came to his house to take care of him. As things progressed, Claude gave him a mandate that he didn't want to suffer. He told him to do what he needed to make sure of that."

Jacques looked away, "Claude was very cold in a way as it related to that. He would analyze himself. How conscious or unconscious he thought he was at each phase. To him, when he got to the point where he was no longer really conscious, and was completely medicated, he wasn't alive anymore. He told me to consider him dead then. 'You don't die when you stop breathing,' he would say. 'You die when you stop being conscious of reality.'"

Jacques smiled and looked at Joe, "Always the philosopher that guy." He shrugged, "So that's how things went. Three years. Phase by phase."

"Was he depressed about what was happening?" Joe asked.

Jacques shook his head, "Not that he shared with me. He never cried or lamented his situation. There came a point where he decided he was going to quit coming to the office. Instead he went fishing more and spent more time with his friends and family. Simple things, but important to him.

"The future of DLGL was important to him too. After the initial diagnosis, we sat on the same wrought iron bench where we always had our talks. I asked him what he wanted to do. I said we could sell the company and he could go spend the money on whatever he wanted. I let him know he could take all the time he wanted too. He didn't have to keep coming in if he didn't want to. He took the time part. Selling the company to someone else he wouldn't do.

"He asked if he could sell it to me instead. Then he gave me the mission of seeing how far we could push this experiment of DLGL. So about a year before he died, that's what we did. He really wanted to make sure it was all clear for everyone. He got his payment and that's what he passed to his family. And the company kept going, which is what he passed to all of us here at DLGL."

Jacques looked away, remembering again, "In that last year, as the disease progressed, he became more and more incapacitated. He was in a bed in his living room and people would come over to treat him. All of us would go see him every day."

"You were there every day?" Joe asked

Jacques nodded, "Me, my wife, my kids." He chuckled, "Claude didn't have any kids of his own. He used to tell me that was because he had to help me raise mine, since I clearly needed help with that. And he did help raise them. We were all as close as any family could be."

Jacques looked away again, "Eventually the disease progressed to the point where he was a fraction of himself. Except for one moment of lucidity the night he died, he wasn't there anymore. So according to his own definition, he had been dead for a long time already.

"And then he was gone. As strange as it sounds, by then, it was a relief for everyone. You're relieved he's no longer suffering. You're relieved his wife and everyone around him is going to stop suffering from seeing him suffer. You suffer still, but in a different way....

"We turned the gym at the office into a funeral home and hundreds of people came to say good-bye. Clients, friends, family, people he'd worked with…"

As Jacques was describing Claude's funeral, Joe's mind went to the day he'd walked Thomas through the museum that had been built for him. He remembered how like Claude, the amount of people who's lives he had touched, had been amazing.

"And then it was over," Jacques said, bringing Joe back to the moment. "And that's when it really hits you. All the people go away. The coffin is gone. And then reality really strikes you." Jacques sighed, "It felt mighty lonely that night. *Mighty* lonely. We'd been friends and business partners since 1972. It was 2001 when he died. That's a hell of a stretch."

Chapter 32

JOE NODDED. ONCE AGAIN HE THOUGHT BACK TO the night when he took Thomas to the museum, and how he'd wheeled him through and then said good-bye.

"You know," Jacques said, "when you're friends with someone that long, and you do the crazy things we did, you have this life full of memories. When we were first business partners in the original company we took an interest in, we bought a building. A school. That was before we formed DLGL. We were with a company called Cogito.

"We were growing like crazy. That was before we understood that growth for the sake of growth could be a not so good idea. So we got tired of paying rent and bought a school. And we had to convert that to an office. We had six partners way back then, so every day at four-thirty, we'd put on our jeans and work boots and we'd work until two in the morning trying to convert this place.

"Tearing down walls with sledgehammers. Putting new walls up. And we did that for months. Saturdays, Sundays....

"One night we were demolishing a stairwell and when we broke the wall we found a bottle of green Creme de Mint and cognac.

The construction guys must have put it there to commemorate the building when they built it."

Jacques paused for a moment and smiled, "At that point, Claude had never taken a drink in his life. He'd been in the armed forces, done all kinds of things, but never taken a drink.

"Well we're tired, and exhausted, and past the point of logical thinking. So I go find a glass and tell him I'm going to show him what a stinger is, and he will remember that name.

"Well the guy has never drank a thing in his life, so he drinks this stinger, and in about seven minutes he's drunk. And then all of a sudden he's sleeping. Then ten minutes later he's up and ready for another one. And he's laughing, and talking about all kinds of craziness…."

Jacques smiled, "We had so many of those crazy things. Those are the adventures that when all of that goes—your business partner, your friend, your neighbor, the guy you can trust with anything, really anything…. It leaves a big hole in your life."

Jacques looked at Joe. "You know what the toughest thing is about losing people close to you, Joe?"

Joe shook his head.

"Not being able to share the good moments. That really is the tough part. That still hurts a lot. Same with when my Dad died. I used to talk to him every day. He'd come over all the time."

Jacques laughed, "I have a habit of getting involved in these manual activities which I am not really good at. But my dad *was* good at them. Plumbing, electricity…. And so whenever I was stuck with something, I'd call him and he'd come and help. We were always working on something in my garage together.

"When he passed away, about two weeks after, I was in the garage. And I was having some kind of problem. So I walked over and picked up the phone to call him and ask for his help. And then it hit me. He was no longer there.

"That was the same with Claude." Jacques shrugged, "It still is. Something good happens at DLGL and I want to pick up the phone or walk over to his office and say, 'You know what? Remember this forecast we made way back when, well it happened.'"

Jacques paused for a moment, "But you know, Joe. In so many ways they're still around. Claude still comes up in our emails in the office. Claude would be pissed, or Claude would laugh, or Claude would be proud. We planted an oak tree in the front of the building to commemorate him. Every time I see it, I think of him. And I know others do too.

"Our VIP product. That was all Claude's vision. And it's the best in the world. There's truly nothing like it. No matter how much money other people have invested trying to come up with something similar. And with every new release, people say 'Claude would be happy to see this.' Or, 'Claude would be proud of this.'

"We have a weekly meeting with our top managers here at DLGL. It's called the OPSCOM meeting. And when we're dealing with a difficult situation, or wondering about something, there are two key questions we use to bring out an answer. The first is—If I was the client, what would I want my supplier to do? And we look at it from that perspective."

"And the second question?" Joe asked.

"If the first question doesn't get us where we want to go, then we ask—What would Claude say?"

Jacques laughed, "By then, that's the twelve pound sledge hammer we're looking for."

He smiled, "So his spirit is still here. It's part of the culture. People even tell stories about him to those who didn't know him. So he lives on."

Jacques looked at Joe, "Can you relate to any of this, Joe?"

Joe nodded. But he didn't say anything. Finally, he took his phone out of his pocket. He looked down and shook his head a little. "I can't delete Thomas' number from my phone," he finally said. "Isn't that stupid? I know he's gone. I know he's not going to pick up. But there's this piece of me that…."

Joe became silent.

Jacques let the quietness fill the space. "I have an idea," he said after a few moments.

Joe looked up, "What's that?"

Jacques got to his feet, "Come on."

Chapter 33

JACQUES WALKED JOE TO A CONFERENCE ROOM ON the same floor where the bar was. It was part of the area where DLGL people and their client counterparts would do work during implementations and strategy meetings. None of those was taking place today, so the area was empty.

Jacques motioned for Joe to go inside. "I have a suggestion for you," Jacques said when they were both in the conference room.

"What's that?"

"I told you how one of the toughest things about losing someone close to you is that you can't talk to them anymore. There are things you want to tell them, share, discuss…but they aren't here."

Joe nodded.

"I'm not saying it's just as good, and I'm not saying it will solve everything going on in your mind. But I think maybe you should call Thomas and just talk to him a bit."

Joe looked at Jacques with a confused look on his face.

"I know you can't *really* call him," Jacques said. He nodded toward a speakerphone on the conference table in the room, "But just try. Just talk to him like he was there."

Jacques shrugged, "Sometimes you just have to get things out. Maybe this will help with that." He glanced at his watch, "It's past five o'clock already. Nobody's down here. You can say what you need to say, or say nothing."

Jacques stopped speaking, and let his comments sink in.

"You saw those broken racquets and hockey stick in the bar?" he eventually said.

Joe nodded.

"Sometimes that's just what needs to happen too. And that's OK."

Joe looked at him, unsure of what to say or do.

"I'm heading out for the night," Jacques said. "Take as much time as you need down here. Just head out whenever you're done. And don't worry if anything gets messed up or out of place. Just leave it. The folks who clean the office will take care of it." He looked at Joe and nodded, "I'll see you on Monday." Then he turned and left, closing the door behind him.

Joe looked around the conference room. It was completely silent, and with Jacques gone, he felt strange and alone. He waited a moment, then took a step towards the door to leave. Then he stopped and looked at the phone on the table. He wasn't sure what to do.

After another minute or two, he sat down at the table. The silence was overpowering. The phone was a speakerphone. He pressed down on the connect button. There was nothing. No dial tone. Nothing. He looked at the back of the phone. It was unplugged.

He sat for a while longer. More silence.

"I miss you, Thomas," he finally said quietly. There was no response. "I feel like I'm just going through the motions most days."

Joe paused for a few moments, "You were my best friend. I don't know who to call anymore when something great happens." He paused again, "You used to kid me all the time about my dates. I always knew it was because you were hoping someday I'd find someone who made me feel the way Maggie made you feel."

Joe shrugged, his voice became more intense, "I go on a date now and I know no-one will kid me about it the next morning."

He paused, "I stand on a stage and present one of the concepts you created and I know I can't tell you how great it went. I can't tell you about the person who came up afterwards and shared some incredible story about the way the Big Five for Life changed them."

Joe looked down, "It's like there's this big hole in my life and I don't know how to fill it."

He looked up, staring at the wall on the other side of the room, "It's not supposed to work this way, Thomas. You were a good guy. You were an honest guy who cared about people." Joe's voice was rising and he was becoming angry. "You did more for people than anyone I know, and you died at age *fifty-five*. There are people who do nothing, absolutely *nothing* for others! They take, they abuse, they steal, they degrade…! And they are still here! Why? Why?"

Joe was yelling now. "How is it possibly fair that someone who did as much for others as you did, dies and those people are still here?"

He picked up a container of pens that was sitting next to the phone. He squeezed it in his hand for a few moments and then threw it. The canister crashed into the wall, the pens flying everywhere. It was satisfying somehow.

"It's not fair, Thomas," he said and shook his head. He was gritting his teeth in anger now. He stood up and took a stack of paper that was sitting on the end of the table and threw that too. "People are supposed to live until they're old! *You* were supposed to live until you were old! Fifty-five isn't old, Thomas! We had adventures to go on, we had companies to build!

"Every time you and Maggie and I would travel together you used to kid me about my wedding. Do you remember? How you and Maggie were going to find out where I was going on my honeymoon and then have room service knock on my door every morning at 6:30 a.m."

Joe was shouting at the top of his voice now, "You were supposed to do that, Thomas! You told me you were going to do that!"

Joe reached onto the table and grabbed a ceramic cup. He thew it against the nearest wall where it shattered into pieces.

Then everything within reach became a projectile. Another cup, pads of paper, post it notes, white board markers, erasers.... They all went flying.

When he was done, Joe collapsed into a chair and put his hands to his forehead. Tears were streaming down his face now. Then he dropped his hands, grabbed the final remaining coffee cup off the table and threw it as hard as he could against the far wall. It exploded.

He was breathing heavily. "It's not fair," he said and shook his head back and forth. "It's not fair."

He lowered his head and stared at the floor. He felt drained. Exhausted. For a few minutes he stayed like that. The anger fueled adrenaline running its course and then leaving him.

Eventually he raised his eyes and surveyed the room. It was a mess. Normally this would have produced some kind of reaction in him. A desire to help. A desire to make things right.... But he felt nothing. Just a deep emptiness. The same emptiness which had been haunting him since Thomas' death.

He got up from the chair, opened the door, and went out.

* * *

Jacques waited until he heard the stairwell door close and knew Joe had left. He nodded his head, "Let's go take a look," he said to Jean-Guy, DLGL's janitor.

The two men had been sitting in a conference room down the hall. In the opposite direction of the stairwell.

Jean-Guy let out a low whistle when they walked into the room Joe had been in. "You were right about this," he said to Jacques.

Jacques nodded. He bent down and picked up a few things from the floor and put them on the table, "Sorry about the mess, Jean-Guy. Do you want some help getting things back to normal in here?"

Jean-Guy shook his head, "Leave it to me. I figured when you asked me to disconnect the phone, take out anything valuable and put all the extra things in here, something like this might be the result. I'll take care of it."

Jean-Guy picked up some of the papers and put them back on the table. "Do you think it helped him?"

Jacques surveyed the room, then shook his head a little, "I'm not sure."

Chapter 34

JOE WOKE UP ON SATURDAY MORNING FEELING THE same as he'd felt the night before when he'd left the wrecked conference room. There was a forest with walking trails near his hotel. He went for a short walk, which turned into hours of wandering.

He was thinking. Sometimes about Thomas' death. Sometimes about his own museum. Sometimes about nothing.

He ate a late lunch, walked some more, and ended up going to bed early, completely exhausted.

The next morning he woke and checked his messages. There was one from Jacques.

"Will be working on the race car this evening. Out at our barn where we keep it. Why don't you come out. I'll be there until eight or so."

He gave the address.

For most of the day, Joe debated whether to go or not. His heart wasn't in it. But he had nothing else to do either. And there was another part of him, from somewhere he didn't really even understand, which was telling him to go. Eventually, he sent Jacques a message telling him he'd meet him out there.

Chapter 35

WHEN JOE PULLED UP TO THE ADDRESS JACQUES had given him, he parked near a small entry door on the side of the building. There was a note Jacques had left for him, telling him to come in. Joe opened the door and stepped inside. As the door closed behind him, he looked around.

The place was interesting. It was definitely a workshop. Parts, equipment, tools…were everywhere. There were a number of race cars in various states of repair.

It was more than just a workshop though. On the walls were pictures of race cars and drivers, plaques, trophies, racing jerseys…. This was a museum of sorts. A history of all the team had been through.

"This is the kind of thing Thomas loved," Joe thought to himself. A place which had an energy. A story to tell. A place where people got inspired by the adventures of others. And in turn, found new inspiration for their own endeavors.

The air inside the shop carried the smell of cars being worked on. Not in a bad way. To the contrary, it was comforting somehow. Like things were repaired here. Put back together. Rebuilt.

"Glad you could make it, Joe."

Joe looked toward the voice. It was Jacques. He was standing next to one of the partially dismantled race cars, about a hundred feet away. "Come on over," he said.

When Joe walked over, he realized there was someone with Jacques. "Joe, I'd like to introduce you to a friend of mine," Jacques said. "This is Yves. He's the genius mechanic who keeps these things running."

Joe and Yves shook hands. "Nice to meet you," Yves said. "Jacques has been telling me about your project with DLGL."

Joe nodded, "It's going to be a great interview when it's all finished."

"Well, I hate to say hello and then good-bye," Yves said. "But I want to get online and see if I can find these parts we've been talking about, Jacques. We're going to need them in two weeks in Mid-Ohio and I'd prefer they get here as soon as possible."

Yves extended his hand to Joe, "A pleasure meeting you, Joe. I hope you'll come by and join us in the pit crew for a race sometime."

Joe shook his hand and nodded, "I'd like that."

"Thanks, Yves," Jacques said as Yves turned and headed for the door. "I'll talk with you tomorrow."

"Nice guy," Joe said when Yves had left.

Jacques nodded, "Great mechanic too. He's been with us for ten years."

"Is that typical? For a racing team to have the same mechanic that long?"

Jacques shook his head, "No, that's pretty much unheard of. Most people don't respect the mechanics very much. They treat them as pretty expendable. Too many egos at play," he said and smiled.

"Personally, I see it a little differently. When I'm behind the wheel of a car going one hundred and eighty miles an hour, I really don't want parts flying off into the wall. Or me either for that matter. I like someone taking care of things who knows the car inside and out and is pretty darn committed to making sure everything works right."

Joe nodded. He'd noticed that about Jacques during their time together. He built long-term relationships. It applied to his employees, his business partners, and as Joe had just learned, to the mechanic for his race cars too.

Where a lot of leaders feel like the people around them should be grateful because they have a job, with Jacques it was almost the opposite. *He* felt grateful to people because they stuck with him on his adventures. And because those people could tell Jacques genuinely cared about them and looked out for them, they continue to stick with him.

Joe looked down at the engine of the car, "What were you guys working on?"

Jacques handed Joe a small spring about an inch and a half tall and half an inch wide.

"Really?" Joe asked.

"Don't let its size fool you, Joe. This little spring has a very important job."

"Which is?"

"It forces up a cap to maintain pressure in the engine cooling system."

Joe smiled, "I take it that's important?"

Jacques nodded, "If this spring is weak, and not doing what it's supposed to, water or vapor will escape from the cooling system.

When that happens, the pressure and boiling point of the water will go down.

"Maybe it starts turning to vapor at 240 degrees Fahrenheit instead of 260 degrees, which is when it's supposed to happen. That may not seem like a big deal, but it is."

Jacques pointed to a particular spot on the engine, "It will probably happen around here, where water is closest to the combustion chamber. A little pocket of vapor will form and it will grasp onto some casting imperfection in the chamber.

"When that happens, things won't be cooling in that spot like they're supposed to. Which creates a problem right here on the other side of the chamber. A little hot spot is going to form, and act like a firing spark plug, before that action is supposed to happen.

"Fast forward a micro-second, and on that hot spot we have a condition known as pre-ignition. A fire has started. Then the spark plug starts a second fire—the normal ignition which was *supposed* to happen.

"Only that's one fire to many. It creates so much pressure and heat, that the whole charge explodes in a sub-millionth of a second, instead of burning progressively. That explosion, which is called detonation, causes parts of the engine to start disintegrating.

"A few more rotations of the piston, and in short order, the engine blows up."

"That doesn't sound good," Joe commented.

Jacques shook his head, "Not good at all. When an engine blows, it often blows holes in the side of the crankcase, which causes oil to spill out everywhere and the car to spin out of control. That's a very bad thing if you're a driver trying to fight for your life to keep your car from slamming into a concrete wall at almost two hundred miles an hour. Also bad if you're trying to avoid getting slammed into by one of the other cars racing around the track at that same speed."

Joe nodded.

"It's also a bad thing for your racing team," Jacques continued. "Because you just lost a very expensive engine. And in the process of the engine blowing up, it blew apart the very expensive carbon fiber which is the shell of the car. All of which means you're going to be out of commission for a while. Plus, you have a very big bill to pay in order to get the car back up and running."

Joe held up the small spring, "All because this little guy didn't do what he was supposed to, huh?"

Jacques nodded, "You can't have weak little springs in your race car. Or weak other parts either. Whether it's four dollar components, or four thousand dollar components, no weak links can be tolerated. Or you pay a big price down the line."

Jacques looked at Joe, "And for the sake of your article—the same thing applies to people in a company."

Chapter 36

JOE HANDED THE LITTLE SPRING BACK TO JACQUES, "What do you mean?"

Jacques shrugged, "Once a humane standard of performance is established in a given culture, it must be met by all. The people who don't meet the standard have to be replaced. Yes, you give them reasonably sufficient amounts of training, coaching, or new roles. There comes a point though, where if they aren't performing, they need to be let go.

"When you've got people giving their best effort, they're intentions are good, and there's an alignment of interests among all the participants, you're poised for success as an organization. But when you don't, and something isn't working out, you need to fix it and fix it fast. Or just like the engine, you're going to blow up at some point."

"Does that ever happen at DLGL?" Joe asked. "Where someone stops doing what they're supposed to be doing and they have to be let go? It seems like with the longevity of your people, their commitment to each other, all the perks...that it wouldn't happen."

Jacques paused for a moment, "It doesn't happen often, but we've still had to deal with it. We recently let someone go who wasn't performing anymore."

"How long had they been with DLGL?" Joe asked.

"Seventeen years."

Joe looked at Jacques in surprise, "Wow! That's shocking. What happened? I would have thought after seventeen years someone would be pretty clued in."

Jacques shrugged, "I think maybe sometimes people stay in a nice place long enough they forget it isn't like that everywhere else? So they sort of take it for granted."

Joe nodded.

"And sometimes people just change. They put themselves in a box. They only want to do certain things. Our culture and method at DLGL is one where you jump in and do lots of different things depending on the situation.

"Client management, support, R&D…. That's part of what enables us to have the culture we do. So if someone makes the decision they no longer like that and only want to do one type of thing… DLGL stops being the right place for them.

"And with a culture like ours, there's no place to hide. If they stop contributing, or they contribute but their attitude isn't very good, people will let them know. Then it's up to me or someone else in management to take action. Which we do."

"How long was this person's performance sliding," Joe asked.

"It was slowly going down for a number of quarters in a row. Then one quarter it went down *a lot*."

"Enough that you called?"

"Exactly. And then it wasn't good the next quarter either. So I started asking people what the deal was. Since the person had been with the company for so long, every effort was made to re-assign them to a different role and give them different opportunities. But when the next quarter wasn't any better, that was it.

"Every possible chance was given for that person to turn things around. When they didn't, they were then the spring which would blow up the engine and wreck the whole car."

Jacques shook his head, "It's never pleasant to have that conversation. But you owe it to all the other people who *are* doing what they're supposed to be doing. And doing it in the right way and with the right spirit. Otherwise, what kind of message are you sending *them*?"

Joe nodded, "That reminds me of a particular client of ours. He learned about the Big Five for Life though one of our events and became very inspired. He was just turning fifty and felt challenged to really evaluate who he was as a leader compared to who he wanted to be.

"We have a process we use to help individuals discover their own Big Five for Life. So first he went through that.

"Then he wanted to clarify the Big Five for Life and purpose of his company. The company had been in business for decades. But like in a lot of organizations, it wasn't all that clear who they really were, and what type of organization they wanted to be.

"So we took him through the process of identifying the company's Big Five for Life and purpose. Then over the next six months, he rolled it out across the organization. About eighty percent of the people had a connection to it. Many expressed that they had been *waiting* for something like this."

"And the others?"

"The others told him in not so many words that it was all a bunch of bullshit. They didn't believe it, they didn't see the point, they didn't want to be a part of it."

Jacques nodded, "What happened?"

"He had some tough decisions to make. Was he committed to creating his version of an incredible organization? The kind of place he was proud of? The kind of place he knew in his gut he was capable of creating and then leading?

"If he was, it was going to mean letting go of some things. Self-doubts about what he was capable of for starters. Followed by command and control management practices which he'd been using for twenty-five years even though he didn't really believe in them. And it was also going to mean letting go of some people who had been with the company for a lot of years."

"What did he do?"

Joe nodded, "To his credit, he sided with his potential, not his fears. He gave people a chance to understand what he was doing and get onboard if they wanted to. When it was clear that wasn't going to happen for some people—he let them go."

"And everyone else asked him why he waited so long to do that," Jacques said.

Joe nodded, "You are *exactly* right. For years, people had been frustrated by those individuals. They had bad attitudes, they were very self-serving in what they did and the way they did it.... The people he let go had been annoying clients and good employees for years. But the leader had been so worried about how the company could fill the gap without them, nothing was ever done. The leader's fear of the unknown was greater than what he perceived to be the size of the problem. So he didn't take action."

"And after he let those people go?"

"Within weeks, productivity leaped in the company. In ways the leader had never imagined. He learned that one of the guys was responsible for about thirty percent of all the mistakes made at implementations the company did. So with him gone, mistakes went down, productivity went up, and client satisfaction went up.

"One of the other guys was responsible for fixing issues once implementations had been completed. He had been hiding countless client issues from the rest of the team. Problems that had been annoying clients for *years*. This guy had claimed they were fixed or he was working on them, but neither was true.

"It took months to fully clean up the messes those people had made. But the positive impact of having them gone didn't take any time at all. When I spoke with the leader, he was adamant about how quickly the energy in the company changed, and how the dynamics among team members was instantly better.

"And the longer term results have been great too. Within a year of making the changes, the company's revenue was up 35%. And another 31% the year after. And they're getting follow-up work at clients, which is something they *never* got before. Probably because of all the problems that weren't being solved."

Jacques nodded, "Clients don't like giving additional work to a vendor who can't even do the current work right. And you're not going to get any referrals in those cases either. But on the flip side, when you do what you do well, and with the right attitude, you are automatically first on the list for those things. That's been one of the keys to our success ever since we started DLGL."

Joe nodded, "I'm thrilled for the leader I was describing. He took on some tough choices and now he's well on his way to having the type of company he really wanted to have. It's been a great story for him."

Chapter 37

THE TWO MEN SAT IN SILENCE FOR A FEW MINUTES. Jacques was working on a part for the car. Joe was thinking.

"You know, Joe." Jacques said after a little while. "It's not just about replacing car parts when they aren't working. Or letting people go who aren't pulling their weight in a company."

He paused for a moment, "There's a lot of that in life too."

He took a rag and polished some grease from the piece he'd been working on. "I'm a straight shooter, Joe. Never been much for holding things back or trying to tip-toe around a topic. You and I have spent a lot of time together over the last week. And I can see you're hurting. I can tell Thomas' death has hit you hard."

He paused again, "Because of what I went through when Claude died, I can understand that at pretty significant level."

Jacques finished cleaning the piece he was holding and put it up on the work bench, "It seems to me though, that there's something out there which maybe even you haven't figured out. Something you're hanging onto even though it might be time to let it go."

Joe took that in. Then he looked away. He was thinking. Finally, he turned back to Jacques, "The board of Thomas' company has asked me to take over for him."

Joe paused, "Thomas set things up so leaders growing up in his original company had the chance to launch companies of their own if they wanted to. He also started other companies and asked people in his original organization to lead those.

"In all of those situations, Derale Enterprises always took an equity stake in the new ventures. It was a way for Thomas to keep his best people together, while still giving them the chance to lead in their own way."

Joe paused, "And the equity stake was just a small piece of it. Thomas set up all kinds of ways for the leaders to stay connected, learn from each other, help each other….

"With Thomas gone, the board is concerned that no one is there to keep those connections going. No one is there to make sure the bonds are not only maintained, but optimized. And it's those bonds which truly makes everything within Derale Enterprises work as well as it does."

Joe shook his head, "They've been talking to me about the role for a few months. I've just kept putting them off. Now I think they're a little concerned whether or not I'm still the right guy."

"Are you the right guy?" Jacques asked.

Joe paused, then eventually nodded his head. "I am," he finally said. "Everyone has gifts. Things they do particularly well. Part of my gift is I see things others don't. Connections. Iterations. How one thing will lead to another and another and another, and something amazing will result. Or in some cases, something not so amazing will result, so a different path should be taken.

"Thomas was like that too. That's what made him so great at what he did. And it's probably part of what made us get along so well.

"He'd call me on a random morning and start mapping out some incredibly synergistic idea between the companies. He could see it all in his mind. Then we'd start throwing ideas back and forth, inspiring each other until the idea had grown even bigger and more amazing.

"When he walked people through it, they were enthralled. He was an artist like that. Creating something from nothing. And people loved him for it."

Jacques nodded, listening quietly. When Joe paused, he decided this was the time. Time to share something he had sensed for days now.

"You know, Joe," Jacques said quietly. "You not taking over for Thomas…isn't going to bring him back."

Joe didn't reply.

"Sometimes people hang on because they're afraid," Jacques continued. "Afraid to take a new job even though they know the current one isn't their path. Afraid to leave a relationship even though they know it's not the right one. Afraid to lead in the way they know they are capable of, because they're afraid of what others will say."

"I'm not afraid to lead," Joe said.

"I know," Jacques replied quietly. "You're afraid to take over for Thomas, because that will mean he's really gone."

Joe didn't want to hear that. He didn't want to acknowledge it. But he knew it was true.

"He's gone, Joe," Jacques said. "And nothing you do, or don't do, is going to bring him back."

Joe felt sadness wash over him. Heaviness. The weight of the reality.

"There were two things which helped me the most when Claude died," Jacques said. "Things which kept me going during the dark moments. The first was that we had created something together. And I knew it was important to him that it kept going even though he wasn't around anymore.

"I believe that's the same with you and Thomas and Derale Enterprises. You might not have been there at the start with Thomas, like when Claude and I created DLGL. But you helped him build it during all the years you've worked together."

Jacques paused for a moment, "I'm not saying you should take over for him if you don't want to. But from what you said a few minutes ago, that role is what you do better than almost anyone else in the world. It's you at your best. I think Thomas would be proud to know that someone was still doing it, and that the 'someone' was you."

Joe nodded, letting that sink in. "You said there were two things," he replied. "What was the second one?"

Jacques smiled, "I picked a few of my favorite Claude memories. Ones that made me laugh. Or admire. Or be grateful that I'd known him.

"When I found myself struggling with his death, I made myself think of those favorite memories. To honor him for being the great person he was, instead of focusing on the fact that he wasn't here anymore."

Jacques chuckled, "I remember one time we had everyone in the company take one of those personality tests. Where they tell you if you're in the upper left box, or the lower right box. You're an introvert or an extrovert, a thinker or a feeler…. When I got my results back, I was right in the middle on everything.

"Claude and I were joking around about it and I told him the results meant I was really adaptable." Jacques laughed, "Do you know what he said?"

Joe shook his head.

"He told me it meant I had no personality."

Jacques laughed again and shook his head, "That was him. That was our friendship. If someone else had said that to me and really meant it, he'd have taken their head off. And I'd have done the same if they'd said it to him. But between the two of us, we could kid each other to no end."

Joe smiled. A small bit of lightness coming over him. "I like that idea," he said. "I like that idea a lot."

He paused for a few moments then looked at Jacques, "Thanks."

Jacques looked back at him and nodded in reply, "You're welcome, Joe."

Chapter 38

JOE WOKE UP EARLY THE NEXT MORNING. HE FELT better than he'd felt in a long time. The more he reflected on the conversations from the night before, the better he felt.

He arrived at DLGL at nine. Today was the day Jacques had his interview with the magazine and Joe wanted to sit in. As Joe came through the doors, he saw Jacques was already in his office.

"Morning, Joe," Jacques said when Joe knocked on the frame to his office door. "Come on in and grab a seat."

Joe put his things on one of the chairs in front of Jacques' desk and sat in the other. "All set for your interview this afternoon?"

Jacques nodded and smiled, "Easy to be interviewed about something you live every day."

Joe smiled back, "Thomas used to say something just like that."

Jacques noticed that Joe had brought Thomas' name into the conversation unprovoked. That was the first time it had happened during Joe's visit. "How are you doing today?" he asked.

Joe thought for a moment and then nodded, "I'm good." He nodded again, "Better than I've been in a long time as a matter of fact."

Jacques smiled, "Glad to hear it." He glanced at his watch, "The reporter called a little while ago and asked if we could push the interview back until eleven. Which is actually a good thing, I think. There's a piece of the puzzle here at DLGL, which you and I haven't covered yet. I planned on going over it with you at some point, and with the interview being delayed a little, this feels like the right time."

Joe nodded in reply.

"My guess is that what we'll talk about in the interview will be more nuts and bolts," Jacques continued. "Specific methods we use here, our approaches to different situations.... That's usually the type of questions I get asked when I do these things. What I want to share with *you* is one of the key foundational elements which makes us successful.

"A reporter doing a quick interview doesn't have the context for what I'm going to explain. They wouldn't get it, because they haven't spent time in our culture like you have. But I know you'll get it. And I think for the people who read your article, this could be one of the most important things they get out of it."

Joe nodded again, "OK. Where do we start?"

Chapter 39

"AS I'M SURE YOU CAN TELL, JOE, WE DO OUR VERY best to create an environment for the DLGL people which is the best possible. Accomplishing that has meant thinking differently. Also acting differently.

"The same has held true for creating a system which is the best possible for our clients. In our industry, most of the major players create and sell a box of software. Now it's a big box. I'll grant you that. You don't get to be the size of an SAP or PeopleSoft without offering a pretty big box. But it's a pre-packaged box nonetheless.

"And this creates a bit of a problem, because every client is different. There are a lot of similarities, but there's also a lot of specific nuances. This is particularly true in anything that has to do with managing people. Because cultures and collective labor agreements can never be fit into an off the shelf product."

"For example?" Joe asked.

Jacques nodded, "Train engineers don't get paid the same way if they're driving a train downhill compared to uphill. A municipal employee is paid with two digit precision for his day job. But if he works some overtime that night selling hockey tickets at the municipal stadium, his overtime is calculated with three digit precision."

Jacques shrugged, "That's two of the thousands of these types of things we deal with. And what's in the box can't address those. So what do you do if you're the company who just bought the box?"

Joe shrugged, "Modify the box?"

Jacques nodded, "Exactly. But since you don't have that expertise in house, you hire someone who can modify the box for you. Which they do. And all is OK…for a while. At some point though, the box gets upgraded to a new version.

"This is now a problem, because no one who makes the box knew about *your* modifications. So nothing in the new version is designed to accommodate those. And the person who did the modifications to the original box has long since gone away."

"Which means you just lost some of your key functionality," Joe interjected.

Jacques nodded, "In our industry, projects cost anywhere from seven hundred thousand up to twenty million dollars. And more than sixty percent fail. In part because of the reasons we spoke of the other day. And in part because no one can figure out the box. Of the projects that *do* get implemented, a few years later once the box is upgraded, no one knows how to make it work."

"Sounds like a huge waste of time and money," Joe said.

Jacques nodded again.

"So how can it be done differently?" Joe asked.

"I'll show you."

Chapter 40

JACQUES GOT UP AND WALKED OVER TO A WHITEboard. On it was a schematic drawing. In the center was a circle with the words "One Single Integrated Database." Surrounding the circle were about forty little interconnected cubes.

"When we get a new client, one of the first things that happens is we spend about six weeks with them. The goal is to make sure we understand *exactly* what they need information for. Where is it going? How is it going to be used? Where does it need to be integrated?

"That's really the whole point of a system like this. To get the right information, to the right person, in the right way. In some cases, that's very straightforward—providing online access to a person so they can see their pay stub online. In other cases, it's a little bit more complex—making sure an employee's direct deposit is spread across multiple accounts in the percentages they wanted.

"Then in other cases, there are *many* levels of complexity. Providing a list to a manager of who should be called in first when somebody is sick. A list which is based on the agreements in a union contract. Also based on who has the proper certifications. Also based on who hasn't just come off a sixteen hour double shift. Also based on where it won't result in triple time pay.

"The output is different, but the goal is the same. The right information, to the right person, in the right way.

"Now, this is not our first time around the block. We've been specializing in this for over thirty years. As a matter of fact, with many of our clients, we understand more about their payroll, accounting, and other HR systems than even they do. Because at most of our clients, people don't stick around like they do here at DLGL. So after eight or ten years, no-one at the client is left who was involved in the original project."

"You're a pillar to your pillars," Joe interjected.

Jacques looked at him quizzically.

"It's an expression we use often in my company," Joe said. "Our pillars are our most important clients. The ones who contribute the most to our bottom line and keep us standing strong. Our goal is to be a pillar to those clients. To add so much value, and to become so structurally valuable to them, that we are a critical piece of the foundation which enables *them* to stand strong."

Jacques nodded, "A great way to think of it. Yes, we become a pillar to our clients. At the start though, we provide pillars to become pillars."

This time it was Joe who gave the quizzical look.

"For most of our competitors, when they get a new client, they assign a team to work with the client," Jacques began. "As we discussed the other day, the team isn't necessarily the most knowledgeable about that client's industry. It's a combination of whoever is currently available because their last project just ended, and new hires.

"Our competitors have a twenty percent employee turnover rate. They need to replace one out of five people every year. So it's pretty likely that not only is the team not all that familiar with the client's industry—the new hires probably aren't all that familiar with the product they're implementing either."

Jacques nodded, "Because of our long employee tenure here at DLGL, we're able to use a different approach. When we get a new client, or pick up a piece of new work at an existing client, we assign the most knowledgeable and experienced people to the work. Which means they are fast. *Really* fast. And it means they are accurate too. They know which questions to ask because they have seen similar projects, for similar clients, a dozen times over the last fifteen years."

Jacques smiled at Joe, "Have you ever taken on one of those home improvement projects? Constructing a shelving unit, installing a ceiling fan, putting together a bicycle for a kid…?"

Joe laughed, "Not so much the last one, but sure, I've taken on some home improvement projects now and again."

"And have you ever noticed that the second time you do it, you know what mistakes to avoid compared to the first time?"

Joe laughed, "Oh so true. That first one is the worst. Slow and lots of re-dos."

Jacques nodded, "Same thing here, only the project is a lot bigger and the mistakes can be a lot harder to fix. Which is why we get the most appropriate person on the project in the first place. Because this isn't the second or third time they've worked on it. It's the twelfth or the twentieth.

"I mentioned to you yesterday, the average tenure of our employees is sixteen years. Not only have we been down these roads before in specialized industries, we've been down them *a lot*."

"But how can you make sure that right person is always available?" Joe asked. "Don't you face the same challenges as your competitors?"

Jacques smiled, "Nope. And when I explain why, I think you'll see why I feel it's so valuable for the leaders who read your article."

Chapter 41

"OVER THE LAST THREE YEARS, WE BROUGHT ON twenty percent more clients. We didn't have to add a single additional person to meet that growth."

Joe looked at him surprised, "Really?"

Jacques nodded, "Really."

Joe thought for a moment, "It seems like that would mean you had a lot of people sitting around waiting for work the last few years."

Jacques shook his head. "Not the case. Here's why." He picked up a marker and drew a diagram on the white board.

"This," he said and pointed to the two thirds area of the pie. "This represents our daily activities. They include designing and implementing solutions for new and existing clients. Plus supporting the clients we already serve.

"Now, because people stick around here so long, and they get better and better at what they do, we keep getting more and more efficient. So a pension project that five years ago might have taken eight hundred people hours, now takes us only six hundred."

"You've built the bookshelf ten times, so by now you're lightning fast," Joe added.

Jacques nodded, "Right. That's one reason. The other reason, is this," he said and pointed to the other part of the diagram. "R&D."

"Research and Development?"

Jacques nodded, "Correct. What happens, is that when people are working with clients, they're getting faster and faster on everything from implementing solutions to fixing problems. So fast as a matter of fact, that they have extra bandwidth. And here at DLGL, that extra bandwidth is applied to R&D. Which includes making our system, our processes, and our support methods, even better and more efficient than they currently are."

Joe stepped back from the board and thought about that for a few minutes. "That's incredible," he said after a while. "You're creating a self-fulfilling prophecy in a good way. By creating an environment where people love to work here, such as the gymnasium, Vipnasium, choosing their own schedule, hockey, and all the rest of it, people don't leave. Because they stay, they become more efficient.

"When they get so efficient they have extra bandwidth, instead of letting people go, you simply shift their efforts to R&D, which ends up making *everyone* more efficient. Eventually, you are in a position where you can take on more and more client work without increasing the size of the team." Joe let out a slow whistle, "That's a heck of a system."

"So," Jacques said. "To your question earlier about how do I make sure the right people are available. If someone's expertise is required, that week they simply shift their weekly allotment of R&D time to the client need we're facing. Then shift back when they're done."

"Is it that easy?" Joe asked.

"Not only that easy, but incredibly efficient. I'll show you."

Chapter 42

"HERE'S HOW IT GOES WITH OUR COMPETITORS," Jacques began. "Let's say they pick up a new client in the banking space. As I mentioned earlier, the consultants assigned to the project don't necessarily have banking client experience. They just happened to be assigned to a banking client because they are available. So from the start, they're not as efficient as they could be.

"Well, lets say there *is* someone within the greater organization who is a banking expert. They've done two or three of those projects. To get them involved in a meeting about a specific design question, or integration issues, means getting on their calendar. Maybe flying them out.

"This is a problem because they're already fully booked up. If they weren't, they would have been assigned to this project initially. So pulling them in, means they have to leave their project to work on this other project. And that means their own project is going to fall behind. *Or*, they'll have to work extra hours to make sure it doesn't fall behind. So they're not all that excited about having to help.

"But let's say you can get them in. Then you have to spend a couple of days getting them up to speed on the nuances of all the changes that have been made at this one particular client. Otherwise, how are they going to be able to understand what kind of an impact their suggestions would have. Finally, when that's all done, they can offer their opinion and go back to their own project.

"Only two days later, when their solution has created two more challenges down the line, what do you have to do?"

"Go through all that again," Joe replied.

"Exactly." Jacques shook his head, "Here it's different. We have everyone in house. Have a banking question? The best people for that are already on the team. Still missing a piece of information? The person with the answer is in the building. Call them up, bring them into the team room and talk it over. Since there are no one-off solutions created by third-party people, there's not the lengthy catching up period required. And since they've been living and breathing the system for sixteen years, the people you're asking for help, know the system inside and out."

Jacques smiled, "We can solve in an hour what would probably take three weeks for our competitors."

"And because you have that built in bandwidth lever with your R&D, pulling that person in doesn't set them back at all on the rest of their work," Joe said. "So they're not as resistant to help."

"Not resistant at all," Jacques replied. "Especially because their bonus is tied to the overall company performance and also to their overall contribution to the entire organization."

"Bonus?" Joe asked.

Jacques smiled, "Let's hold the bonus discussion for later. We'll get there though, I promise. For now, yes, you're right. The R&D lever is part of what enables us to move resources around immediately and do more with less for our clients."

Joe smiled back, "You mentioned there were two things. What's the other one?"

Chapter 43

JACQUES POINTED AT THE SCHEMATIC AGAIN. WHERE the cubes surrounded the circle of data. "The strength of a system is in the integration. How effectively can one piece of effectiveness be applied somewhere else? Can every part plug and play with every other part? To what degree does a piece of brilliance ripple throughout the entire system so that the single piece of brilliance ends up being exponentially more brilliant?

"When our competitors supply a box to a client, there is always something which needs to be customized. Always. So as I mentioned before, the client hires a third party vendor to create that customization. And it might be some great work. Hundreds of thousands if not millions of dollars worth of effort.

"In their world, the only one who gets the benefit of that, is the one client."

"And then only until the next version of the box comes out," Joe said.

"Exactly."

"And with DLGL?"

"At DLGL, when we build something for a client, it is owned by DLGL. When it's something which would benefit the majority of our clients, we incorporate it into our overall system. At a minimum, we make it available as an option for clients who would benefit from it."

Joe looked at Jacques with surprise, "Really? So let's say I'm a client and I spend a million dollars to have DLGL create a new piece of technology to use with my information. Every other DLGL client immediately gets the benefit of that? I would think that might upset some people."

"Sometimes we have to do some explaining," Jacques replied. "But they get it quickly."

He went to the whiteboard, "First of all, you were going to spend the million dollars anyway. Whatever the technology is, it provides a value that exceeds the million dollar cost, or you wouldn't be doing it."

Joe nodded, "True."

"Second of all, yes, you contribute that piece of technology to the system overall, which means others get it for free. But what do *you* get for free?"

Joe nodded, "Whatever everyone else is paying to create." He pointed toward the whiteboard, "I get it. I can either invest my million and get a single thing worth a million dollars. *Or*, I can invest my million and not only get *my* technology, but have access to *all* the technology DLGL is creating for their other clients too."

Jacques nodded, "Exactly. Your million dollar investment gets you everything you asked for. Plus another ten million worth of technology selected for *your* particular needs, from a library of many tens of millions worth."

"Some of which I may not need," Joe said.

"Some of it you might not," Jacques replied. "On the other hand, some of it you may not even *know* you need. Or you didn't even consider having built for you, because you thought you couldn't afford it."

Jacques smiled, "A big part of what we end up doing for our clients is helping them grow into capabilities they didn't even know were available. And which they couldn't have afforded if they were investing in each and every technology on their own."

Joe whistled, "So if I'm that client, I'm pretty happy about my million dollar investment."

"There's one more reason to be happy," Jacques said. "A very big reason."

Joe smiled, "Which is?"

"What happens when there needs to be a change to your system? A new government regulation comes out which impacts payroll. Or a completely new technology enters the market, like tablets or devices. Something which changes the way you want to access information and do business?"

Joe looked at the schematic for a moment. He thought through the different scenarios they'd been discussing. Then he whistled again, "Whatever change you make is guaranteed to ripple through the system. Since it's been integrated from the start, and the same people who designed it then created the modifications, and handled the support, the changes automatically ripple through the system."

Jacques nodded, "Those are the reasons we can effectively take on twenty percent more client projects without adding a single additional person. And you know what I'm convinced of Joe?"

Joe shook his head.

"That if a leader really thinks about it, these same concepts can be applied to almost any industry."

Chapter 44

JOE STOOD AND STARED AT THE WHITEBOARD AND the schematic. He wanted a few minutes to reflect and process all they'd been talking about. Jacques' explanations had been so simple and yet so profound. Joe felt like he was staring at a crystal somehow. Each piece perfectly shaped, connected, and integrated. Pieces which were impressive on their own. And when viewed as a whole, were something truly beautiful.

He realized that it went beyond the beauty of the system, too. Although a crystal of its own, it too was connected. To the culture, the people, the building, the philosophy.... Everything was connected.

It was overwhelming to the point where Joe couldn't quite wrap his mind around it all. Yet he knew it was something spectacular nonetheless.

As he sat there, his mind spinning, he knew the example of what DLGL was, had the potential to inspire a lot of leaders. Ever since joining Derale Enterprises, Joe had been involved with sharing great ideas with great leaders. It was one of his primary roles within the organization. And he had seen the way those already great leaders would incorporate the new ideas into their own teams, divisions, and companies and take them to even higher levels.

He knew if he could get his own head wrapped around exactly what he was looking at here at DLGL, and then explain it well, the ripple effect would be huge.

Chapter 45

JACQUES' PHONE RANG. HE PICKED IT UP AND SPOKE for a moment, then hung up.

"Our interviewer is here," he said. "Louise is bringing him in. His name is Gilbert Morin, from *Excellence*, one of the top business magazines in the country."

A few moments later, Louise arrived, escorting a well dressed gentleman. After introducing him, she left.

Jacques shook the man's hand and said something in French. The man replied, also in French. Then Jacques turned toward Joe, "Gilbert, I'd like you to meet a friend of mine. This is Joe Pogrete. He's working on an article of sorts as well. So I thought it would make sense if we all talked things over together if you don't mind."

"I don't mind at all," the man replied in English. "Nice to meet you, Joe. I'm Gilbert Morin."

Joe smiled, "Nice to meet you too."

"Shall we then?" Jacques said and indicated toward a table with three chairs.

The men sat down.

"So what can I do for you, sir?" Jacques asked Gilbert.

Gilbert smiled, "I'm on a hunt, Jacques. A hunt for the secrets of DLGL. Our readers saw the results from the rankings last month. Once again, DLGL not only won the best employer in the province, but best in all of Canada. Our readers want to know what you do, so they can try and do it in their own companies."

Jacques smiled and spread out both his hands, "I'm all yours."

Gilbert took out a pen and pad of paper. "I'd like to start by talking about how you find great people, Jacques. What type of process do you go through to recruit the best talent and get them to work here at DLGL."

Joe was interested in hearing this for his own article. It was something he hadn't asked Jacques about yet.

Jacques paused for a moment, thinking of what he wanted to say. "We don't really recruit *anyone*," he replied. "Not in the traditional way where you're out there at schools getting fresh graduates, or trying to entice people away from where they're at. It sort of works the opposite way for us. We get a lot of unsolicited inquiries from people who want to come work here."

Jacques got up from the table and went over to his desk. He opened a file drawer, grabbed a thick file, and brought it back to the table.

"This is what I'm talking about," he said, and passed both Gilbert and Joe a few of the letters from the folder.

The men scanned them quickly. Gilbert smiled and held up the first one he'd read, "This is quite amazing. She says she knows you're not hiring, but she read about you and DLGL in a magazine and has always wanted to work in a company like it. She's asking if you would keep her information on file and if you ever need someone like her to let her know."

"That's pretty typical," Jacques said. "People hear about us through articles, or when we win awards. The truly motivated ones send us letters like that."

He smiled, "We got one once from a woman in Australia. She'd read an article about us and said she would be willing to move all the way from Australia to Montreal. That's a heck of a compliment."

"Do you ever hire the people who write you letters?" Gilbert asked.

"Sometimes," Jacques replied. "First, we always respond with a very nice letter thanking them for their interest. We let them know we'll keep their information on file, and if we need someone in the future we'll let them know. And yes, although we don't do a lot of hiring these days, there have been times when we went back to that file and contacted people."

Jacques thought for a moment, "I think one time it had been three years since they'd sent the letter. Another one might have been even longer than that."

"And they were still interested?" Gilbert asked.

Jacques nodded, "The ones who were writing for all the correct reasons, still valued those reasons. So yes, they were still interested. I don't think anyone who sent us a letter and then we made them an offer, has ever said no."

Gilbert scanned the other letters he was holding, then handed them back to Jacques. Joe did as well. "So you really *don't* recruit people," Gilbert said. "You don't have to because people are trying to get *your* attention."

Jacques nodded, "Recruiting isn't something we need to spend our resources on."

"You said you don't do a lot of hiring," Gilbert said. "What's your annual turnover."

"Zero," Jacques replied.

Gilbert looked at him with surprise, "Zero?"

"We've occasionally had to let people go." Jacques nodded to Joe, "Like the case we were talking about last night. But our average annual turnover is zero."

"How often do you hire new people?" Gilbert asked.

Jacques thought for a moment, "Not very often. The last person we hired is a full time personal trainer for everyone here at DLGL. She works in our Vipnasium."

"Vipnasium?" Gilbert asked.

Jacques described the Vipnasium and the logic for having it. At Gilbert's prompting, he then spent another ten minutes explaining many of the other amenities which were available for the people at DLGL.

Joe was watching Gilbert. He could tell he was surprised by what he was hearing.

When Jacques was done, and Gilbert had finished writing his notes, Gilbert looked up, "That's really amazing." He thought for a moment, and then tapped on his notepad. "But I'm confused about something, Jacques. A few minutes ago you said you don't hire very often. And the last person you *did* hire wasn't part of your core business. Are you not interested in growing?"

Jacques smiled, and Joe knew something good was coming.

Chapter 46

"WE HAVE A VERY SIMPLE PHILOSOPHY AROUND growth," Jacques began. "We want to be as small as possible to both afford R&D and keep kicking our competitor's asses."

Gilbert and Joe both laughed.

"So you haven't grown in a long time then?" Gilbert asked.

"Well, growth is measured in lots of different ways," Jacques replied. "The amount of clients we serve has grown. Our revenue and profits have grown. But to accomplish that we have not had to grow our employee count, or the physical size of our company at the same rate."

Jacques looked at Gilbert, "You said you were on a hunt, right?"

Gilbert nodded.

"Here's a big piece of the treasure. One of the most important questions a leader can ask is how big do they want their organization to be, and why? People creating a business always seem to be caught in this whirlwind of growth. So they end up doing things without doing them right. Hiring is an example of that.

"They get a new client. They need someone to service the client. They don't have a lot of time to look for someone, and so they hire whoever they can find.

"And I get it. When you're small and competing against big companies, it can seem tougher to attract great talent. But that's where your value proposition comes in."

"Value proposition?" Gilbert asked.

Jacques nodded, "As a leader, have I taken the time to clarify who we are as an organization? What our purpose is? Who we serve and why? Can I articulate where we're going and what we want to accomplish? Those things are what inspire people to want to be a part of your organization. And if you don't have them, you end up with employees who are just there because they needed a job and you had one available.

"Part of that discussion about who you are, your purpose, where you're going...is deciding what role size is going to play in your organization. Do you want to be the biggest? Do you want to be the biggest but in a particular niche or region? Are you willing to sacrifice quality for growth?

"And a factor associated with that, is what kind of timeline are you thinking about? Are you in this to build a long-term company? Or are you planning on creating something and selling it off?"

Jacques paused for a minute to let all that sink in, "If we wanted to be the biggest at DLGL, that would change everything here. Absolutely everything. We'd have a bunch of sales people knocking on doors. We'd go public and get a bunch of money. We'd talk to venture capitalists. We'd get implementation partners who don't care about the end result but just want to get the job invoiced.

"It would be very different. *Completely* different."

Gilbert smiled and finished writing something on his notepad, "That is treasure, Jacques. Very powerful. So because you've created a culture where people want to be here, you get very motivated people at the start. That same culture inspires people to stay, so you develop deep expertise and higher productivity per person. That enables you to grow in the areas you want, without growing in the areas you don't want."

Jacques nodded, "Exactly."

Gilbert looked at his list of questions, "Jacques, on our initial phone call when I asked you about doing this interview, you mentioned the long tenure of people here at DLGL. And how critical that is to the company's success. On average, people have been here sixteen years and you've got a number of folks who have been here for more than twenty.

"How have you kept people from getting stolen away by one of your competitors or your clients over all those years? It seems like with all the success you've had, other companies would be really interested in attracting your people away."

"We make sure that can't happen," Jacques said with a smile.

Gilbert smiled back, "What's your secret?"

Chapter 47

"WE'VE TALKED ABOUT SOME OF IT ALREADY," Jacques began. "We create a good environment. The building, the lighting, the free food, the gym, the Vipnasium.... All of that is a big part of it. Also, as we've talked about, people have flexibility in their schedule. Knowing you can arrange your life so you can drop your kids off at school or pick them up after school, is a big deal.

"Also, we assume competence until proven otherwise. Which translates into people being trusted to do their job, without someone constantly watching over their shoulder.

"All of those put us at the very top of the pyramid in terms of what other companies could offer. There's only a couple of other levers a competitor could try and pull."

"Money?" Gilbert asked.

"Yes and we take care of that by paying above market wages. And our bonus plan is better than anyone else's."

"Bonus plan?" Gilbert asked.

Jacques nodded, "Each quarter there are opportunities for everyone to pick up special bonuses. Sometimes they are individual, like the bonus recently attained when Sylvie, our last smoker, quit.

"Other times they are spread across the company. Like the fifteen thousand dollar bonus next time we replace a competitor's implementation."

He smiled, "And then the biggest bonus, which is consistently in play, is the one which is tied to our overall performance each quarter. Financial results, new clients, things like that."

"Is everyone eligible?"

"Absolutely. That's the whole point. If people aren't collectively aligned, you end up with little fiefdoms and power bases. With our plan, either we all win, or we all lose."

"How is the bonus distributed?"

"It's paid out the first nine weeks of every quarter following the results."

Gilbert nodded, "Why not spread it out over the entire quarter?"

Jacques chuckled, "Because no matter how much we are all dedicated to what we're working on, we all have human brains and human tendencies. And one human tendency is that when something is always there, the risk is you start to take it for granted.

"That applies to the weather, the way people treat their spouse, people's health…. By only distributing the bonus the first nine weeks of the quarter, a good thing happens. That tenth week, when everyone gets their paycheck and the bonus isn't there…it's very obvious and a good reminder that the bonus is a big deal.

"It keeps all of us on our toes a bit. Keeps us appreciative."

Gilbert smiled and made a few notes.

"In addition to the above market salary and bonus, we also have a very generous retirement plan," Jacques said.

"We initiated the pension plan shortly after we started the company. We were so small back then that we had to beg a big insurance company to manage the funds. The way the plan works, is that after someone has been with DLGL for three years, they can start contributing up to four percent of their salary. That grows half a percent each year up to eight percent. The company matches what they put in.

"With a reasonable return on our investments, and reasonable increases in people's salaries, in another thirteen or fourteen years, the fund will exceed a million dollars per employee. That's pretty good considering most of the people here are in mid-career at this point."

Gilbert took more notes and then looked up. He smiled.

Jacques smiled back, "What is it?"

"There's this trend in what I see here at DLGL," he said. "It's this attitude of doing things well. *Exceptionally well.* I would expect that from a company whose been in business for thirty years and who I know from doing my research has such long-term relationships with their clients. The extent to which you've applied that approach to everything else impresses me a lot though."

Jacques shrugged, "If you're going to do something, do it right. Having a great product isn't enough. It's all connected. The way we treat each other, how people are rewarded, the environment here at DLGL. Our success comes from *all* of it being done right."

Gilbert nodded, "I see that."

"Which is a good lead-in to one of the most important pieces of the whole picture which we haven't covered yet," Jacques said.

"Which is?"

"PEC."

Chapter 48

"PEC?" GILBERT ASKED.

Jacques nodded, "PEC. It stands for Peer Evaluation Component. Here's the thing. You've commented about our pursuit of an excellent system here. You're right. We're constantly asking ourselves how we can make this whole DLGL experience better. For our clients, for our partners, for ourselves...."

"Part of our solution is in what we just talked about. Making sure everyone is financially rewarded when we collectively do well. That helps keep everyone rowing in the same direction. But about twenty years ago, we discovered that the reward wasn't enough. The system could be improved. Because it's not enough to reward people for the collective result if they don't have a say in making the collective effort better."

Gilbert looked at him confused, "I'm not sure I follow you."

Jacques nodded, "Imagine I told you that you'd receive a fifty percent bonus on your salary if as an organization we hit our goal. But you had no way to voice your input on whether people around you were pulling their weight or not. At some point, that would be a problem. If people weren't contributing, you'd have no way to change it. You would just get more and more frustrated and it would eventually demotivate you.

"So that's where PEC comes in. Four times a year, everyone here at DLGL evaluates everyone. The janitor, the support people, our receptionist, me.... We all evaluate each other.

"It's anonymous, and feedback is only given on a global basis, like what the overall average is. Or, when people have gone up a sizable amount, or down a sizable amount."

"Why not give feedback to each person?" Gilbert asked.

"Because it's less about the specific number in relation to your peers and more about the movement," Jacques said. "You don't want someone getting in a huff because they came out a 7.6 instead of a 7.65. And last quarter they were a 7.7, so what changed? Keeping it where feedback is only done in the extreme situations, avoids all that.

"What we tell everyone is to do their best. If you do your best, the results will show what the company overall thinks of your best. You may not like or agree with that result, but if you're doing your best, then it doesn't really matter. It is what it is.

"Right now we are in a period of extreme stability. The lowest average PEC is 7.73. The best is 8.98. Our average overall is 8.11."

"Do you have a specific number you use for the 'sizable amount' you mentioned earlier? That merits individual feedback?" Gilbert asked.

Jacques nodded, "A movement of up or down .2 either way, and it's time for action."

"Which is?"

"If it's in the down direction, I pick up the phone, call the person up, and tell them their PEC is down .2 or .4, or whatever it's down.

Then I tell them I have no idea why it's down, but I'm sure they do. Please fix it. Then I hang up."

Gilbert laughed, "That's it?"

Jacques shrugged, "That's enough."

"And if the movement is in the up direction?"

"I call them up, tell them their PEC is up .2, .4, or whatever it is. Then I tell them I don't know exactly why, but I'm sure they do. Keep up the good work. Then I hang up."

Gilbert laughed even more, "Short and sweet, huh?"

Jacques shrugged again and smiled, "It works."

"How long do you give people to make changes if their score keeps declining quarter by quarter?"

"Usually the first phone call fixes it. People know. Maybe they've been particularly grumpy lately because of something at home. Or they've gotten into a beef with someone and it has created a problem. They know. And once it's apparent that PEC is showing it, they know they better fix it.

"If things keep moving downward, we make every effort to move the person elsewhere within the company to some other role which would be a better fit. Or we help address whatever issue might be creating the problem.

"No one gets fired because of the PEC. They get fired for a variety of reasons which led to the PEC being what it is. But the PEC saw it coming.

"And that makes exit meetings, when they *are* necessary, very simple. It's not just 'stupid management' who thinks you should leave, or that you aren't contributing. Its everybody. You were warned, you were given chances to fix it, and you didn't."

Jacques shook his head, "Those conversations are *very* few and far between. But when they happen, that's how it goes. As a frame of reference, anytime someone in the past has had their PEC drop below 7.3, they ended up either leaving on their own, or we let them go."

Gilbert nodded, "It seems strange. You have such a long average tenure. I have a hard time envisioning a situation where someone would suddenly get so out of sorts they bother enough people to make their PEC go down. You'd think they'd get it together."

"It doesn't happen very often," Jacques replied. "A handful of times in the last thirty years. But it does happen. People are people and sometimes they do strange things. And sometimes they've been here so long they don't remember what they have. We've had people leave and then try to come back once they spend a little time in other places."

Gilbert wrote a few notes, then looked up, "Do you have a copy of the PEC scoring sheet, Jacques? I'd like to see what the rating scale is based on."

Jacques nodded. He got up from the table and grabbed his laptop off his desk, "Let me show you on here."

Chapter 49

GILBERT LOOKED AT THE SCREEN. ON IT WERE THE names of individual employees and a scale from one to ten next to their name.

"All you do is go line by line, person by person, and click the number you think is right for them," Jacques said. "It takes just a few minutes and everything is done confidentially. Then the software tabulates all the answers, and here in the dashboard section, the leader can see all the results."

"Including which phone calls you need to make," Gilbert said and pointed to a little phone icon next to some of the names.

Jacques nodded.

"That's really sharp," Gilbert said. He looked at the scoring sheet again and pointed to the text at the top. "The instructions are really interesting."

At the top of the scoring sheet, was the following:

The PEC addresses effort more than absolute results. Expected results are already built into people's base salary. What you are evaluating is goodwill, trying hard, espousing the group objectives, being pleasantly available to help out others, being a team player, having a genuine interest in the client's service, paying attention to quality.... Basically, the things we espouse as an organization. This is not about whether or not you like or dislike someone's lifestyle, so keep that in mind.

Jacques nodded, "Initially, people pushed back on those instructions. They wanted something more specific. But the whole point of having an aggregate score is that it's *aggregate*. For one person, their reference point on a particular co-worker might be as simple as whether or not someone is friendly in the hallway or break room.

"For someone else, their reference point might be how well that same person performed on a project the two of them have been working on for the last twelve months. So you get a wide spectrum, which works out perfectly."

Gilbert looked at the screen again. Next to the numbers were a few additional guidelines.

10 points -Best rating. Excellent. Beyond the call of duty. Perfect, or other words to that effect.

8 points -Very good. Better than average. Some room left for improvement.

7 points -Average. Normal elsewhere. Room for improvement.

5 points -Not very good presently. Will probably change.

3 points -Bad. Things need to change soon.

1 point -Very bad. Won't change. Should not work here.

n.o. -No Opinion. For individuals where you do not have an opinion, n.o. should be indicated.

"The goal was to keep it simple," Jacques said. "And this does that. We've tweaked it over the years a bit, but by and large, this works well just as it is."

"How many n.o. results do you get?" Gilbert asked.

"We let everyone know it's normal that they're going to have a few. But don't become lazy. You don't need perfect absolute knowledge of someone to have an opinion. Just make sure it's your own opinion and not something you picked up from somebody else."

"So PEC fills that need you mentioned earlier," Gilbert said. "This gives people a way to provide input when their co-workers are doing great and not doing great. This gives them a voice."

"People always have a voice," Jacques replied. "Someone could come talk to me or any of the other senior folks at any time and share what's on their mind. But yes, this gives them another outlet, and a confidential one. And again, as an organization it gives us a look at what the *aggregate* voice is saying."

"Do people take PEC pretty seriously?"

Jacques nodded, "They do. In large part because people have a deep desire to see DLGL do well. It's also one of the three components we use in determining each individual's quarterly bonus. So that adds another level of importance to it."

Gilbert paused for a moment, "So having a quarterly PEC really helps create the culture here at DLGL. And that in turn helps create the success."

Jacques nodded, "The collective group will be very tough on someone who is not contributing their fair share. So by its nature it helps people stay focused, contribute…be nice."

"Be nice?" Gilbert asked.

"Sure," Jacques replied. "Maybe your only interaction with someone is you see them when they arrive first thing in the morning. Your PEC assessment is going to be based on that interaction. Are they friendly? Do they smile and say hello? If they're a grouch, you're going to reflect that in your PEC score for them. So it helps everyone remember to be nice."

Gilbert wrote some more notes, "I really like that," he said after a few seconds. "I can see where it's a powerful tool on a lot of fronts." He paused again, "When did you implement PEC?"

Jacques thought for a moment, "We put it in place early on when we hit about twenty-five people. It was obvious we needed something, so we came up with PEC."

"What did people think when you announced it?"

Jacques laughed, "Well, we tied it to a new bonus we announced, so that probably helped." He paused and became more serious, "The truth is, people want to contribute. They want to make a difference. PEC helps them do that. I think the only thing I'd have done differently is to implement it even sooner."

Chapter 50

GILBERT FLIPPED THROUGH HIS NOTES, "JACQUES, I know you said with the way you've chosen to focus, and your low turnover rate, you don't need to hire a lot of people at this point.

"Clearly hiring right has been something you've done well along the way, or you wouldn't have been as successful as you are. Can you give some advice to those leaders who *are* out there actively hiring? Maybe ones who are earlier in the life cycle of their company, or replacing people for some reason?

"You mentioned earlier the importance of being clear about who you are as an organization—your purpose, where you're going, and what you want to accomplish. Let's say a leader does all that. What about the actual hiring process. What should they look for in a candidate?"

Jacques sat back in his chair and put his hands behind his head. "The selection process is quite important," he said after a moment. "You want to bring in people who are available for the value proposition you have. Because not everyone is going to be.

"For example, this surprises people who don't know us, but part of our success has come from not bringing in massively driven, over achievers."

"Really?" Gilbert asked.

Jacques nodded, "Someone like that isn't really available for a common definition of a purpose. Or a common definition of success either. Instead, they'll have a personal definition of those things, which will override everything else. So although they may do some great things at the start, they'll end up breathing everyone else's oxygen at some point.

"As we've been talking about, our success and growth comes from the long term success of *everyone*. Not just a few individuals. For someone who's determined to be a rock-star, the collective success of *everyone* isn't generally the value proposition they're interested in. They want to stand out."

"What do you do in an interview to see if someone *will* be a good fit for the organization's value proposition?" Gilbert asked.

Jacques smiled, "I watch for it." He chuckled, "When people have been with DLGL for ten years, we host a ten year jubilee. They get a chance to make five thousand dollars for a ten minute speech about their journey here at DLGL. And almost every single one talks about their initial interview."

Gilbert smiled, "Why is that?" What do you do?"

Jacques shrugged, "Mostly I explain who we are, the way we think, and what DLGL is all about. Then I look for reactions. I try to figure out if the person is really available to buy into what I just shared with them. I won't stop until I have an opinion on that."

Gilbert nodded, "Are you looking for visual cues, verbal cues, just followings your instincts? How do you know?"

Jacques shrugged, "I just know. I've had people look at me and I can tell they're thinking I'm nuts. I see it in their eyes. One time

I was interviewing a candidate and shared that we don't have many people getting divorces at the company.

"The person just looked at me like I was crazy to be mentioning something like that in an interview. So I explained I wasn't saying we were the *reason* for the low divorce rate. But at the same time, we don't create situations that put people under the kind of stress that *will* break up families.

"We're not creating families or holding them together, but we're not breaking them apart. We're staying out of the way. Which is generally our policy on family affairs. We don't have people working seventy hours per week. Thirty-five or thirty-seven is just fine. That gives them plenty of time to take care of the rest of their life."

Jacques laughed, "I sort of shake my head when I read about companies with dry cleaning services, and concierge services for their people. I mean it's great if they're *also* telling people to not overdo it with the work schedule. But otherwise, those things are just a way of justifying why it's OK to keep people there at all hours of the day. A way of keeping them in the office.

"Why not just let them go home and take care of what they need to take care of? Maybe see their kid's soccer game, or have dinner with their family."

Gilbert nodded, "So the person you were talking about. They thought you were a little crazy when you brought all that up, huh?"

Jacques smiled, "I could just tell they weren't sure what to make of it. So of course I went *further* down that road. I asked how *they* saw it, what *they* thought…. Eventually it was clear they weren't going to be a good fit."

Jacques laughed, "Actually I think it was one or the other of my two favorite criteria which made it clear the person wasn't going to work out."

"Which criteria are those?" Gilbert asked.

"I explain to interviewees that we are looking for people who are available to be happy. Then I ask them if they are available for that. If they are, I explain that we won't screw it up."

Gilbert smiled, "Isn't everyone available to be happy?"

Jacques shook his head, "Everyone here at DLGL is. Or they wouldn't be here. But outside of here, no, I wouldn't say that everyone is available to be happy. Their belief systems about themselves, life, what's fair, what isn't.... The way they make their choices.... A lot of people make choices which are designed to sabotage their own happiness. And in a group setting, they'll sabotage the happiness of others too. That's not the kind of person you want in your organization."

Gilbert wrote more notes on his pad, "Available to be happy. Got it." He looked up, "You said it might be one of your two favorite. What's the other one?"

Jacques leaned back and smiled, "Now that I'm thinking about it, I'm pretty sure this one was actually the deal breaker for that candidate. I like to explain to people that we're looking for someone who is coming here to die."

Chapter 51

JOE BURST OUT LAUGHING. "SORRY," HE SAID. "DIDN'T mean to interrupt. That's hilarious though."

Gilbert laughed too, "What exactly do you mean when you tell them that, Jacques?"

"We're not looking for people who are only interested in sticking around for two years, getting some experience, and then going somewhere else. We don't want to be a *step* along the path. We want to *be* the path.

"People who work here are interested in learning, doing different things, challenging themselves.... So it's not that we are asking people to do the same thing every day. To the contrary, actually. We don't want someone who wants to do the same thing every day. That's not how our model works. We *do* want someone who wants to be part of something for a long time though. Because that *is* how our model works."

Jacques smiled, "So I explain to candidates that we are looking for someone who is coming here to die. Then I explain what that means. And I watch for their reaction."

Gilbert wrote more notes, "I really like that," he said. After a few moments, he looked up, "Jacques, has it ever not worked out with someone? They looked like a good fit in the interview and then weren't once they joined the company?"

Jacques shrugged, "No matter how hard you try, every once in a while someone will fool you into believing they are open and available for what you are proposing. But it quickly becomes clear it's not going to work out. And once it's clear, you need to act right away.

"I hired someone one time, and when they came in for the first day of work, I basically didn't recognize them. They were dressed completely different, acted completely different." Jacques shook his head, "It literally was like a different person from the one in the interview."

"How long did they last before you let them go?" Gilbert asked.

"Four days."

"Four days?"

Jacques nodded, "Four *very* long days." He smiled, "That was when we were quite a bit smaller and also the person was working directly with me. And I knew. And once you know, you've got to take action right away." He shook his head, "Ooh la la that was a mistake." He laughed again, "And everyone has been pulling my leg about it ever since."

"Why was it so important to correct things that fast?" Gilbert asked.

"Because it's not fair to everyone else," Jacques replied. "People here take great pride in what they do. It's more than just a job to them. This is a big piece of who and what they are. It's not fair to them to let someone do a half-ass job.

"Also, as we discussed, our bonus plans let people share in the overall success of the organization. So it's not fair to let other people suffer financially because you allow someone to not pull their weight."

Jacques shrugged, "People don't expect everyone to be a hero or a genius. That's not it. They do expect everyone to try as hard as everyone else. That's all."

Jacques shook his head a little, "Ignoring a problem doesn't make it go away. It just eventually turns the little problem into a big problem. As a leader, you're going to have to address it at some point. It's much easier and much more effective to do it right away and all the way to completion.

"If you don't address the issue of a non-performer right away, you'll eventually lose your best performers because of it. Then you've got huge problems.

"And on the flip side of that situation, if you don't reward people for doing things well, you'll lose good people too. That also is a *huge* problem.

"We talked about PEC earlier, that's one of our greatest assets for knowing who's performing and who's not, and then rewarding or letting go as appropriate?"

Chapter 52

GILBERT HAD FILLED PAGES AND PAGES OF NOTES. Joe could tell he was really intrigued by all he was hearing.

"Jacques, I've got enough to fill five interviews, so I want to thank you already for all you've shared," Gilbert said. "One of the things I love to put in the end of my interviews is just a few brief take-aways for readers. Some quick suggestions they can apply in the way they lead, or even the way they think about their business.

"I've been capturing some things you've said already and put them in that slot. Such as 'Know how big you want to be, and why.' And, 'Know who you are, why you exist, and what you want to accomplish.' Can you think of anything else you'd like to share that fits into this 'quick hits' category?"

Jacques thought for a few moments. "Maybe something like this," he said. "Invert the value proposition."

"What do you mean by that?" Gilbert asked.

"Well, most leaders, and really most organizations, make decisions based on what's in it for *them*. But at DLGL, we've found that when we put our people first, and then our customers, and we wrap all of that into a proven business model, the profits naturally follow.

It's a byproduct of focusing on our people and our customers and doing right by them."

Gilbert noted what Jacques had said.

"In conjunction with that, I'd say treat everyone with respect. Your clients, customers, vendors, employees of *all* levels…. Everyone is a fellow human being. So treat them with respect."

"Those are great," Gilbert said. "Do you have a couple more?"

"Don't move with the masses unless they happen to be going where you want to go," Jacques said. "And that applies to people's personal life as well as their business. We've gotten to where we are because we're willing to think and act differently. Not *just* for the sake of being different. But because we've realized that by doing it different, we can do it better."

Gilbert wrote that down.

"I guess this next one goes along with thinking differently," Jacques said. "If you're going to bother doing it—do it right." He paused for a moment, "Whether it was designing our building, creating our pension plan, deciding how much equipment should go in the Vipnasium…. I never saw the point in doing a half-ass job just so I could say it was done. If you're going to do it—do it right."

Jacques paused for a moment, "This next one is something which has guided me well in many different situations. If you want things to go well, get an alignment of interests. When you're clear about what you want, and you take the time to find out what other people want, and then you align those things…you can do anything." Jacques shook his head, "In the absence of that alignment, you're going to end up with everybody looking out for their own self-interest."

Gilbert wrote more notes and then looked up, "These are great, Jacques. Do you have one more for me?"

Jacques thought a bit, "I recently read an article talking about executive compensation. Most executive's salaries and bonuses are based on two things—revenue and headcount. They aren't based on profitability and turnover rates.

"The thinking is, if a company has a lot of top line revenue growth, and is also growing its employee count, it should be making more money. Which is ridiculous, because that often isn't the case."

He shrugged, "So what you end up with is people making decisions in the best interest of their personal bank account and not in the best interest of the organization."

Jacques smiled, "Did you guys ever hear the story of the snake and the guy in the rowboat?"

Gilbert and Joe both laughed and shook their heads, no.

"Well this is the right time for it," Jacques said. "There's this guy out fishing in a little row boat. And he hears this knocking on the side of the boat. He looks down and sees this snake which has just grabbed a frog and is preparing to eat it.

"The fisherman feels bad for the frog, so he reaches down and takes it out of the snake's mouth. Well, the little frog hops merrily away, but the snake looks all sad. So the fisherman takes out a bottle of fine cognac that he has with him, picks up the snake, and gives him a little shot of it. Then he puts him back in the water to swim off.

"About ten minutes later, the fisherman is busy fishing and he hears another knocking on the side of the boat. He looks down, and there's the same snake with another frog, and he's lifting up his head to give it to the fisherman."

Gilbert laughed. Joe too.

"You get more of what you reward," Jacques said. "You reward people for having a lot of employees and you get a lot of employees. You reward people for top line revenue, you get a lot of top line revenue. So if you're not getting what you want—change what you're rewarding."

Gilbert was writing quickly, to capture what Jacques had said. When he was done, he looked up and smiled, "Great stuff Jacques, great stuff."

"Enough hunting for now?" Jacques asked with a smile.

Gilbert nodded and smiled back, "Enough for now."

Chapter 53

JACQUES WALKED GILBERT OUT TO THE LOBBY. THEY spoke for a few minutes, and then Jacques returned to his office. When he walked in, Joe was writing furiously on the white-board.

"Something from the interview spark an idea, Joe?"

Joe smiled and continued writing, "It was great information. I appreciate you letting me sit in. We've covered some of those topics already, but it was good to hear it a second time. And for a lot of the other questions Gilbert asked, they were things I was curious about too, so I'm glad he asked them."

Jacques looked at what Joe was writing, "And this?"

Joe finished and stepped back from the white-board. "Over the last few days I've had this sense of something. After you and I spoke this morning about the way you use R&D, the sense was even stronger. And it kept growing as you were answering questions during the interview."

Jacques nodded.

"But now I think I have it," Joe said. "At least the first version of it." He stepped back from the white-board and looked over what he'd written.

"There's some brilliant math just waiting to be done, which would really demonstrate the power of this," Joe added. "That's something I'll work on. For now though, here's the essence of it.

He pointed to one section which had DLGL at the top. "Your team here is remarkably productive. Because you've created an environment where people want to stick around, your brain power doesn't leave, and that enables you to get better and better at what you do.

"So in essence, you've created a situation where you get exceptionally proficient at going from point A, to point B, to point C. In all the different ways in which that's represented in your business. Which is something that could never happen in an environment of high attrition where people are leaving frequently, and therefore never attaining that high level of proficiency.

"Then you add onto it, this amazing method of continuous improvement through the R&D process you've created. It's not just that you've optimized getting from point A to point B to point C as fast as possible. You're also constantly figuring out ways to go directly from point A to point C.

"All of which is enabled by so many of the different things we've talked about ever since I got here. Including your willingness to allow this R&D gap time where people aren't working directly with clients, but are instead figuring out these improvements.

"Where I come from, at Derale Enterprises, the teams are remarkably productive too. We also have very low turnover and a lot of longevity, so our brain power is maintained also.

"The way in which we inspire that is different though. For us, it's the focus we give to making sure the life purpose of anyone who is hired, is aligned with the organization's purpose. Then we make sure there's a direct link between what they do every day and their Big Five for Life.

"Sometimes that's obvious. For example, maybe one of their Big Five for Life is to create new and interesting things, and part of their job involves designing new outdoor gear for hikers. Other times it's every bit as much of a direct link, but not necessarily as obvious.

"Maybe one of their Big Five for Life is to make a difference in the lives of others, and their role at the company is phone support. We help them understand that by providing great customer support on our phone lines, they truly are making a difference in the lives of the people they help.

"And sometimes, the only link to one of their Big Five for Life is that working at Derale Enterprises in some way enables them to do, see, or experience it when they aren't at work."

"For example?" Jacques asked.

"Maybe our flexible schedules allow a mom or dad to pick their child up every day from school. Or our sabbatical policy gives someone the chance to go on a four week jungle trekking adventure every year. Or maybe it's something as basic as the money they get paid enables them to pay for skydiving lessons.

"The point is," Joe continued, "our high productivity comes from constantly making these Big Five for Life connections and making sure people understand them."

Joe pointed to the DLGL on the white-board again, "What you do is really effective. And especially from a process perspective, we don't do a lot of that.

"What we do is really effective too. And from a Big Five for Life perspective, it's not something you do a lot of."

Joe paused for a moment, "So I guess what I can't help but wonder, and what gets me really excited…"

"Is how powerful would they be together," Jacques said.

Joe nodded and smiled, "Exactly."

Chapter 54

JOE WAS ALONE IN HIS HOTEL ROOM. AS HE SAT AT the desk, his mind was running through the events of the last few days. There had been some amazing high points. Great museum day moments. There had been some low points too. When the darkness and depression had threatened to overtake him.

His mind brought back a memory of Thomas. Over the last seven months when that would happen, Joe would push the memory to the side. But he remembered what Jacques told him in the garage. About honoring Thomas by remembering him in his finest moments.

The particular memory his mind recalled now, was the television interview Thomas did before he died. At the end of it, he had held up two simple little diagrams. Each had an X and a Y axis on it. In the first diagram, there was a curve which simply went up and down. On the second was a curve which climbed.

Joe picked up a pen sitting on the desk and sketched out the first diagram.

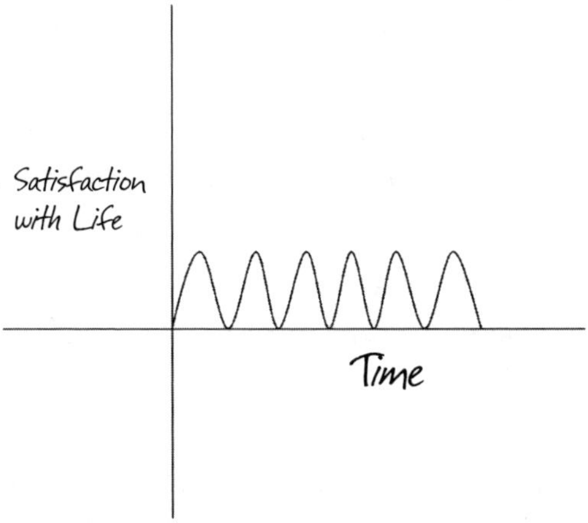
Satisfaction
with Life
Time

When he was done, he looked at it for a few minutes. Then he sketched the other diagram.

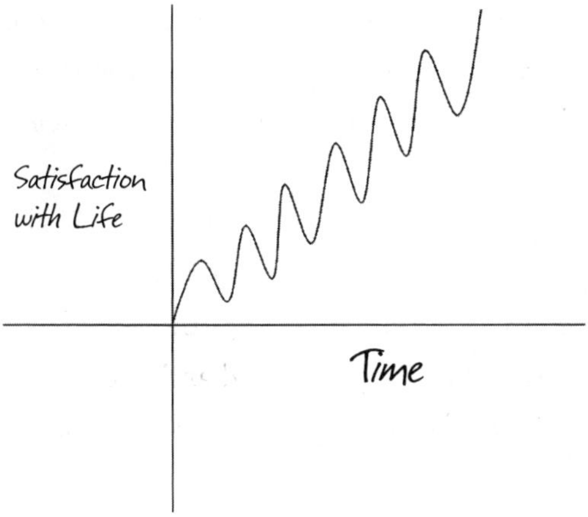
Satisfaction
with Life
Time

As he looked at the drawings, Joe could hear Thomas explaining them.

"...one of life's greatest secrets, which is also one of the greatest secrets of leadership....

"For most people, this is how they go through life. On the X axis is time, and on the Y axis is satisfaction with life. And this basic sine curve—the up-and-down lines that looks like little hills and valleys—represents their life. Over the course of their life, they have highs, and they have lows. But in general, their highs are about the same high, and their lows are about the same low. They just oscillate between these two points.

"The secret to life is to have a sine curve that doesn't just go on over time, but that ascends over time. An ascending life curve. You see, for a person living like that, they don't just oscillate between a set of highs and lows. They keep reaching new highs.

"Everybody has lows. It happens. Even when you're on the right journey, and heading in the direction you want to go, there are still lows. But the point is, when you're on an ascending life curve, at some moment in time your lows are now higher than what used to be your highs.

"And the way to do that is actually very simple. The more moments of your day you spend on something that fulfills your purpose—what I refer to as Purpose For Existing. And the more moments each day you spend on your Big Five for Life—the five things you most want to do, see, or experience during your life.... Then the more your life curve ascends.

"And as easily as we can apply this to our own life, and guarantee it is a success by our own definition of success...it is just as easy to apply it to our roles as leaders. Because being a successful leader is simple. You just need to understand these simple little diagrams, and then apply them."

"Bring people into your organization whose purpose is in alignment with the organization's. Put people in positions where they get to fulfill their Big Five for Life simply by doing the job the company needs done each day. And teach them to do the same for the people they lead.

"When we do that, we're helping people's life curve ascend. And in the process, they're helping the organization's life curve ascend. Because just like a person, an organization has a life curve too. And when the life curves of both the organization, and the people in the organization, are ascending—that's the sign of a great leader."

Joe reached out and picked up the diagrams. He held one in each hand.

"I'm sorry, Thomas," he said as he looked at the one where the curve did not climb. "This is what I've been doing since you died. There are highs, and there are lows, but I haven't really allowed myself to climb."

Joe paused and was quiet for a moment, "I've just been standing as still as I can in the hopes that if I don't move, then one day I'll wake up and you'll be here again. We'll laugh like we used to. We'll keep creating new ideas together for everyone at Derale Enterprises. I'll take you and Maggie on another trip to some crazy adventure spot I found...."

Joe put down the first diagram. He held the second in his hand and looked at it.

Satisfaction with Life | *Time*

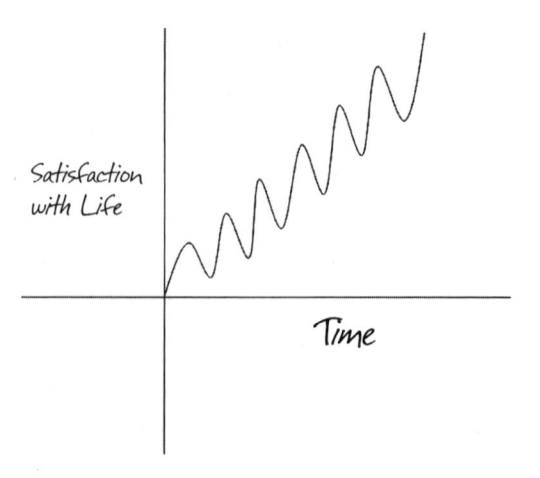

"I would have spent my whole life not climbing if I hadn't met you, Thomas. I owe you so much. And I'm sorry that over these last seven months I forgot what you taught me."

Joe nodded a little, "I'm ready to start climbing again, my friend."

Chapter 55

OVER THE NEXT HOUR, JOE WROTE. IT WAS THE FIRST time in a long time he had let his mind be at ease, and his thoughts truly flow. When he was done, he read through what he had created.

Dear Maggie,

I'm sorry. I'm sorry that over these last months I haven't been the friend I should have been. I'm sorry I haven't been there for you when your own loss is so much larger than my own. We've known each other for a long time and I value all you mean to me and the friend you are.

Since Thomas' death, I've had a hard time coming to terms with it. Finding meaning in it. I know you know that. And I know that's why you sent me up here to spend time with Jacques.

When I was not there as a friend for you, you still were there for me, and I will be grateful for that the rest of my life.

I cannot say I will ever fully understand why Thomas' path required him to leave when he did. But as I sit here now, I have begun to find a peace that over these last seven months I didn't think I'd find.

Tonight I had a flashback to the last interview Thomas did. It reminded me of the way he taught. The way he inspired. And all I learned from him.

The following is for you, Maggie. I hope that in some small way, it helps you as you find your peace.

Your grateful friend.

Love,

Joe

Why?
Why are they gone?
Why did this bright light go out?

There are so many lights who live on. Lights who don't shine nearly as bright. Why did this one go out?

Because when the bright lights go out, we notice. We notice how much light they shed in the world. The way we glowed when we were in their presence, and the way they made others glow too.

We realize how much of a difference they made because they chose to glow so brightly. And we are reminded of how much of a difference we can make too, when we allow our own light to shine.

When they went out, they reminded us that we will not glow forever either. They reminded us to do the things which make us feel alive and make our own light shine brightest. And to do those things now, not wait.

They reminded us that when we shine brightly, we inspire others to shine brightly too. The same way we felt inspired, when we were in their light.

They made the ultimate sacrifice by allowing their time here to end, and their light to go out. They did that for all who knew them. Because when they went out, we were reminded of all these things.

So let us shine our light brightly. Let us honor these gifts this bright light has given us.

Love in a way that lights the life of another. Shine brightly on someone who needs hope. Tell the other bright lights in your life how much they mean to you. Use your gifts in the way that makes your own light shine brightest.

This bright light has gone out, to remind the rest of us that we too are bright lights.

This bright light has gone out, to remind the rest of us...to live.

Chapter 56

JOE WALKED INTO DLGL. THERE WAS A LIGHTNESS IN his demeanor that hadn't been there in a while. He walked over to Jacques' assistant, "Good morning, Louise."

"Good morning, Joe. How are you today?"

Joe smiled and nodded, "Better than I've been in a long time, thanks."

Louise smiled back, "That's great to hear." She looked towards Jacques' office. "I'm sorry, Jacques won't be in until later today. Do you need him for something?"

Joe shook his head, "No, it's OK. Just had some good news and wanted to share it."

She nodded, "Are you going with him to the event tonight?"

Joe looked at her quizzically, "I'm not sure. Which event is it?"

"He's one of the presenters at a conference about finding the best talent. It starts at six o'clock this evening."

Joe nodded, "That's right. I forgot. He mentioned it to me last week. Somehow the days have gotten away from me. I didn't realize that was this evening already. Yes, I plan to go with him."

"Well, if you'd like me to get in touch with him before then, just let me know. Otherwise I know he plans to be back here around three-thirty and then leave from here to the conference."

Joe nodded, "OK, sounds great. I'm going to start putting the framework around the article he's been helping me with. Is there any place in particular I can work for a while which won't be in anyone's way?"

"I'm sure anywhere you'd like is fine," Louise replied. "If you want, you can use the conference room by Jacques' office."

Joe nodded, "Sounds good."

"I'll show you there," Louise replied and got up from her desk.

When they walked into the conference room, Joe looked around. Like all the other places at DLGL, it was well lit with natural light and had a comfortable feel to it. He glanced to his right and noticed the wall was actually a large whiteboard. "Perfect for mapping things out," he thought.

He started to turn away, but something caught his eye. On one section of the whiteboard was a large 'A' written in blue. Covering the 'A' was a clear piece of plastic which had been screwed into the whiteboard, so the 'A' couldn't be erased.

Louise saw Joe looking at it. "Has Jacques not shared that story with you yet?" she asked.

Joe shook his head. He had a vague recollection of something in the Big Little Book of Emails, but he couldn't remember what it was. He was about to ask her about it, when someone knocked on the door frame to the conference room.

Louise and Joe both turned, it was Luc Bellefeuille, one of the senior folks at DLGL. Joe had interacted with him a few times during his stay.

Luc smiled at the two of them, "Hi Louise. Hi Joe. Sorry to interrupt. Just looking for a room to have a quick meeting in a little bit."

"I was going to use this for some work," Joe replied, "but I can find other space."

Luc shook his head, "No, that's OK. No problem. I'll grab another room."

"Luc, can you spare a minute before your meeting?" Louise asked. "I was just about to explain to Joe the meaning of the 'A' up there on the white board. But to be honest, you would be the perfect person to tell the story, since you were in the thick of it the day it happened."

Luc nodded and entered the room, "Sure. I'd be happy to. Although I think he'd get an even more complete picture if we both tell the story. You have your own special perspective on it because of what happened at the end."

Louise smiled, "OK. You start and I'll jump in where it makes sense."

"This story would mean more after you'd been here a while longer, and become even more immersed in our culture," Luc began. "Because it really does say so much about not only *what* happens within these walls but the *way* it happens." He smiled, "But hopefully we'll do it enough justice you'll see how powerful a moment it was.

"As you've probably noticed during your time here, this is a special place. And this special place is full of very talented people who work their magic every day to serve our clients.

"This has not gone unnoticed. Jacques individually, and DLGL as an organization, have won many awards. Jacques has been asked to do lots of interviews, we've picked up very big name clients from our competitors.... And as a company we've been very successful financially.

"With all that in play, it happens that at some point someone decides they would like to own a piece of you. Or even *all* of you. That's where the 'A' on the board comes in.

"A few years back, one of the big players in our industry offered to buy us out. There was a lot of money on the table. And the way Jacques and Claude originally structured the company, if it was ever sold, fifteen percent of the purchase price would be distributed to the employees."

"That's generous," Joe said.

"Well, Jacques would tell you it's being fair," Luc replied, "because it's the employees who have built DLGL. I won't go into the exact specifics of the offer," he continued, "but it was big. *Very* big. For Jacques and his family they'd be set for life. For all the folks at DLGL, none of us would have ever had a mortgage anymore.

"After we received the offer, Jacques told everyone in the company what was going on. Then he gathered me and three of the other senior leaders to talk things over. In that meeting, he shared that in his mind, there were three options for DLGL.

A. Stay as we were.
B. Go public.
C. Take the offer and sell.

"We talked it over for about six hours. Weighed each of the different options at length. Eventually, Jacques told us he would let us make the final decision. We had helped him build the company and should be the ones who decide.

"He suggested we take the night to think it over and let him know our answer in the morning." Luc smiled, "But it didn't take that long. We knew what we wanted. And we knew what the other people in DLGL wanted too. So we told him right then and there we wanted 'A'."

Louise looked at Joe, "Jacques shared with me something you told him about. The concept of museum days." She looked up at the 'A' on the board, "That was a museum day here at DLGL, and especially for Jacques. I remember when Luc and the others told him they wanted 'A', and when I talked with him afterwards."

"What happened?" Joe asked.

She smiled, "He got a little teary eyed, which you don't always expect from someone who when it's required, can be a tough guy like Jacques. And I remember him saying what a special day it was. That you build something and you grow it, and when all your efforts are validated like they were that day…it really is something special."

She smiled again, "Jacques and the leadership team spread the word throughout the company that we were staying as we were. And that night, when Jacques went to leave…."

Joe looked at Louise. He could tell something emotional had happened. Even after seven years had passed, the memory of it still choked her up.

"That night, when he was about to leave, there was a knock on his door." She indicated toward a small metal bucket on the center of the conference room table. It had a quaint little sign on it—Bucket for Bucket Drops. "That's Jacques'," she said. "From a little book called—How Full is Your Bucket? It challenges you to fill your bucket with what matters in life—drop by drop.

"The first person who knocked on his door, brought the bucket from the conference room into his office and put it on his desk. Then one by one, people from DLGL came into his office and put little notes into the bucket for him. They were lined up all the way down the hallway, waiting for their opportunity."

Louise paused a moment. There were tears in her eyes. "There were notes of gratitude, memories, messages about what DLGL meant to them...."

She paused again, "Later on, I watched him go through the notes—one by one. I saw his reactions and what the notes meant to him. It was a very special night. A night which he will be the first to tell you he'll never forget."

Luc looked up at the board where the 'A' was, "The next day, Jacques had that piece of plexiglass put over the 'A'. So as a culture, we would always remember."

Chapter 57

LOUISE AND LUC LEFT JOE ALONE IN THE CONFERence room. He looked at the 'A'. "Such a powerful story," he thought.

He had the Big Little Book of Emails with him because he'd wanted to reference back to some of the emails as he was working on his article.

He opened it up and searched for the one about the 'A'. In a few moments he found the email and read through it. At the very end was a final thought from Luc.

Saying yes to this offer would have meant DLGL disappearing. All of us would become employees, anonymously dissolved within their organization. And this I could not stand. Our culture and our quality of life would go away with them. They would not adapt to our standards, we would downgrade to theirs.

"Preserving our unique culture and having a chance to live in it every day has too much value. Going to work with joy every single day is way more precious than money. This is truly what has guided me on all this."

Joe finished reading the last line of the email and looked up. There was such a wonderful sense of connectedness within DLGL.

It was a common trait he'd seen in all the great companies he'd done interviews at.

There was something in the email Joe hadn't understood. He wondered if Louise could explain it. Just at that moment she walked in the room. "Joe, something has came up and I'll be leaving in about fifteen minutes to take care of it. Do you need anything before I go?"

Joe smiled, "You have perfect timing, Louise." He motioned toward the email he'd been reading. "I was just reviewing the story of the 'A' in the Big Little Book of Emails. Here in the middle it says something about a plan in the event Jacques passes away. That sort of confused me. Do you know anything about it?"

She nodded, "Everyone at DLGL does. Information flows very freely here. Jacques makes a point of keeping everyone up to date through regular emails about what's going on."

Louise indicated toward the book, "The plan the email is referencing is an example of how Jacques feels about this place. About all of us. See in Canada, when someone is the owner of a company and they die, the government requires that their heirs pay a death tax. It's based on the value of the company.

"So in the case of DLGL, the better the company does, the more challenging it would be for Jacques' heirs to keep it going once he passes away. Because they would be forced to pay this large tax bill.

"In most cases, the only way heirs would be able to come up with the money to pay the taxes, is to sell the company. That goes against Jacques' dream that the company and the culture keep going after his death. So he's been forced to take on some financial burdens while he's alive, so that everyone at DLGL will still have their jobs after he passes away."

Louise thought for a moment, "I don't think there's a specific email about 'The Plan' in the book, but I know the information is mixed in there at some point with one of the emails. May I?" she asked and indicated toward the book.

Joe handed it to her and she flipped though the pages.

"Here we go," she said after a few moments. She handed Joe the book and pointed to a particular section in one of the emails.

Joe quickly scanned the text. Toward the bottom, he found what he was looking for. Jacques was explaining why people sell their companies.

d)-they can't afford the taxes upon death if they don't sell the assets before that.

This does not appear to be crystal clear to everybody. So let me give you an example. You bought a house twenty years ago for $100,000. Now it's worth $200,000, and you are fifty-five years old. You figure that when you die, say age seventy-nine, it will be worth $400,000. No problem, there are no death taxes on a residence.

But if that was a second house that you bought and rented out, you would be looking at a capital gains tax on $300,000. Let's say an even $100,000 in taxes. Where do your heirs get the money to pay that? Since it's a house, maybe they can get a mortgage and pay the taxes out of the mortgage money. If not, they would have to sell the house just to pay the capital gains taxes.

When what you own are shares in a corporation, you can't get a mortgage. You could maybe sell the shares, but that would likely be at a huge discount, because it has to be done quickly.

So, people sell their corporations ahead of time for reasons of liquidity upon death. Or they bring the company public. Which is in essence, selling it to the public.

We decided against going public when we got our buyout offer a number of years ago. So, we need another way to face the liquidity needs that will be there when I die.

We have two methods for that which are currently in place.

1. An insurance policy bought many years ago, which started off with a non tax deductible cost of $35,000 per month. That gives you an idea of the magnitude of the required effort.

2. DLGL profits are uploaded to our holding company and are invested in liquid assets. Things like shares of publicly traded corporations. This liquidity will enable the required funds to be available when the time comes. I manage those assets. It takes a lot of time. As much and maybe even a little more than my time spent on core activities here at DLGL.

As you can see, in deciding not to sell or go public, there were some ramifications. If we had taken those options, I would have cashed out my money and financial questions would be irrelevant. Since I wouldn't be involved with running DLGL or managing the assets as described above, I'd also have all my time.

But that wouldn't be the best fit for me. I'm happy that we collectively decided to pay the price to keep DLGL under current managerial practices. We keep it as is—a fun place to work, and even a harbor in tough personal times, which a number of us have gone through.

What we do is without comparison. I like that. I fully enjoy working with people who know this business inside and out, with incredible detail and precision.

That said, we are in the process of testing to its full extent, the continuity in management of DLGL so that it does not rely on the existence of any one person. Which certainly includes me. And it is working out.

So, in a nutshell, the plan is that I be irrelevant to the destinies of DLGL, both financially when I die, and managerially when my brain fades.

Until then though, I'll be an active member of OPSCOM both because it's one of my favorite parts of the week, and because I think I continue to add value. And I'll continue to be involved wherever it makes sense in the rest of the business.

Friday night we are celebrating what makes all this possible: stability, continuity, loyalty, experience, competence. Let's have a good party.

Jacques (Jag) Guénette
DLGL

"Wow," Joe said when he'd finished reading. "That's quite a demonstration of commitment to what goes on here."

Louise nodded, "He loves this place. He loves these people." She smiled, "Sometimes so much that he has to calm himself down a little."

Joe smiled, "Such as?"

"Did you see the message he sent out the last time we won the award for Best Employer in Canada?"

Joe shook his head.

"As you may have noticed, one of the things that makes Jacques, 'Jacques', is he has this interesting combination. It's a mix of the love he has for this company and the people who make it what it is. Combined with a desire for perfection within his approach of choosing one's own imperfections. And to top it off, a willingness to speak his mind."

She laughed, "Let me find the message for you." It took her a few moments of flipping through the Big Little Book of Emails and then she found it. "Here you go," she said.

Chapter 58

JOE LOOKED AT THE BOOK AND BEGAN TO READ.

From: <j@dlgl.com>
To: "DLGL" <DLGL@dlgl.com>
Cc:
Subject: Best Employer

Just finished going through the Watson Wyatt report, the one where we got 2.99 out of 5 on the "feedback from my boss" question. And the report goes on and on about what we should do to better this situation, like proper talent management, which is necessary for a corporation which wishes to participates in excellence growth, and on, and on....

So I guess we have to give in to your wishes and the council of those consultants.

Next week, we will appoint for each of you something new—a boss. From now on, you will deal with the rest of the organization through that boss...after proper authorization from that boss.

That boss will evaluate you every three months, and that evaluation will replace the PEC as the basis for raises and bonuses.

So you better be polite with that boss, because that boss will be the only person who evaluates you from now on.

We are quite a flat organization, so many of you will not be the boss of anybody. So your opinion on the performance of others will no longer be required.

Any request to change bosses will have to be channelled first through that boss of course. No end runs please.

We expect that these changes from PEC to bosses will in time create a more normal turnover rate in personnel. (since boss issues are the most frequent reason for leaving a company).

We'll probably be in the twelve to fifteen percent range. So we will need to hire eighteen to twenty-four percent more people. This will compensate for the useless twelve percent who just came in and know nothing, and the fifteen percent who will be totally inefficient because they spend so much time training and retraining the new hires.

This will mean twenty five percent more office space for all these people, a hiring department with a big budget, etc.

Of course, these additional expenses will be more than our profits, so we will have to cut deeply into some of the niceties that we now have. Things like the bonuses and the pension fund, which are subject to profitability, will be hit first. The Social Committee which runs all our extra curricular activities will now be funded exclusively by the employees. The dental program benefits will be examined in detail for ways to cut costs.

And who are we anyway to afford Christmas parties when our clients can't. It will be good marketing to suffer as they do....

The floor where the Vipnasium is, will unfortunately will be leased to recuperate some revenues, and the new twenty-five percent of office space will be built in the garage. So say good-bye to the driving range and washer and dryer we use for the hockey gear.

Of course I am just kidding. But I am pissed (in case you could not tell yet) on this subject.

WE ARE AN ORGANIZATION BASED ON SELF DISCIPLINE. IF YOU ABSOLUTELY NEED A BOSS TO TELL YOU WHAT YOU ALREADY KNOW ABOUT YOURSELF, OR TO TELL YOU WHAT TO DO, IT WILL NOT HAPPEN HERE. AT LEAST NOT ON MY WATCH.

I EXPLAINED HOW OUR EVALUATION PROCESS WORKS TO A GREAT NUMBER OF HR CONSULTANTS OF ALL SORTS. UNANIMOUSLY, THEY THINK IT IS A WINNER.

I EXPLAINED IT TO THE FOLKS AT WATSON WYATT AND ASKED THAT THE QUESTIONS BE CHANGED BECAUSE THEY DO NOT FIT THE WAY WE EXIST. THEIR QUESTIONS ASSUME A HIERARCHY, WHEN WE ARE A MATRIX.

THEY SORT OF AGREED, BUT THEY CANNOT CHANGE THE QUESTIONS WHICH ARE ALL THE SAME ACROSS THE WORLD FOR WATSON WYATT STUDIES. THEY INDICATED THAT WE SHOULD USE OUR HEADS IN ANSWERING THESE QUESTIONS.

SO, WHEN A QUESTION ASKS HOW OFTEN YOU GET FEEDBACK FROM YOUR BOSS, AND YOU DO NOT HAVE A BOSS, YOU'RE ANSWER IS GOING TO BE WRONG NO MATTER WHAT IT IS. IN THAT CASE, WHY SELECT AN ANSWER WHICH MAKES US LOOK BAD?

These questions and our inability to apply them to our reality lead these consultants to the conclusion that we are not very good at talent management. That is absolute bullshit. Having the right person in the right place is our strongest point.

How otherwise are we achieving the incredible results we are getting in each area as measured by any yardstick from any angle. And it is unfair for all of us.

We still won with a blasting 4.60 average out of 5. Congratulations.

Jacques (Jag) Guénette

Joe finished reading the email and laughed.

"I know," Louise said and smiled. "When you know him, and you know all he does for the people here, and how much he cares, it's funny."

"And I would assume that cleared up the issue of how to answer boss related questions on future questionnaires?" Joe said and smiled.

Louise laughed, "Yes, I think we scored much higher on that one when we won again this year." She smiled again, "That's him. That's who he is. Intense, driven, passionate…. And at the same time, curious, thoughtful, caring, and incredibly protective of his people."

"Not to mention, mixed in all that somewhere is a good sense of humor," Joe said. "I've noticed that already and it's there in that email too."

Louise nodded, "That too."

"One of the things I've noticed as I've done these interviews with different great leaders is they all have a style which is uniquely them," Joe said. "The traits you just mentioned are almost always there. The way in which they display them though is always unique and personal."

He paused for a moment, "That always inspired me. Because it made me realize that great leadership could have so many different faces. It wasn't a closed club of some kind. Everyone has the potential to be a great leader if they want to be. The formula is there for anyone to follow. So many others have demonstrated it and continue to demonstrate it. All a leader needs to do is follow the formula in the way, and with the style, that is uniquely their own."

As Joe said the words, chills ran down his arms. For him, that was the ever present indicator he had discovered something very important for his own life. He shook his arms a little.

"Are you OK?" Louise asked.

Joe looked at her, "Yeah," he said with surprise in his voice. "I think I just remembered something important. That's all."

Louise nodded and glanced up at the clock, "I've got to head out. Are you joining Jacques for the OPSCOM meeting this afternoon? It starts at three-thirty. I would guess Jacques will go right from there to the event this evening."

Joe nodded, still thinking about his comment on leadership and what it meant for his own situation. "I am," he said after a moment. "I'll be there."

Chapter 59

JACQUES ARRIVED BACK IN THE OFFICE A LITTLE after three.

"Getting everything you need for the article?" he asked, as he knocked on the door frame to the conference room where Joe was working.

Joe looked up and smiled, "Hey Jacques, how was your morning?"

Jacques came in and sat down in one of the empty chairs. "Productive. Had a few personal things to take care of. Those are all done. Now I can focus on the OPSCOM meeting, and the event tonight. I hear you are joining me for both of those?"

"If that's OK," Joe replied.

"Perfect. OPSCOM will start in about twenty minutes in here."

Joe looked up at the whiteboard, "Earlier today, Louise and Luc were kind enough to tell me the story of the 'A' up there. I just came across a follow-up email about it in the Big Little Book of Emails."

"Which one?" Jacques asked.

Joe started to read out loud.

From: <luc.bellefeuille@dlgl.com>
To: «DLGL» <DLGL@dlgl.com>

Cc:
Subject: Four years ago today....

Exactly 4 years ago today, was held a very long and emotional OPSCOM...

Jacques announced he had received an extremely substantial offer by someone who wanted to acquire DLGL. Something very strategic that comes once in a blue moon.

That offer would have meant many millions for Jacques, and significant amounts of money for many of us at DLGL.

But it also would have meant the end of DLGL as we knew it... dissolved in the big corporate buyer.

We were given the final decision to accept or to refuse....

An extremely intense meeting took place. We looked at all possible angles, bouncing every scenario, trying hard to make the best decision for everyone at DLGL and their families. This included financial aspects of course.

We also silently reviewed in our minds other things. All that Jacques and Claude had envisioned when they started DLGL. What we have lived through as a group. Our history, our culture, everything that we have built and that we cherish....

And also, just as important, what our future would be if we sold. How confident were we in our ability to preserve all this together, and continue to see DLGL evolve like it has always done?

When the vote took place, Option A was the unanimous decision. We all wanted the adventure to continue as we believed it could here at DLGL.

Four years after, we still enjoy Love, Peace and Fun every single day we wake up and come to work. We enjoy a quality of life like nowhere else, the privilege to work for the best employer, and all in an exceptional environment.

We have all received many bonuses along the way. Those gradually catching up to and surpassing what the distribution from the buyout would have been. From a business standpoint, we have been navigating our way with success through the storms that have hit the marketplace.

And with the release of 8G soon, our future remains extremely bright and exciting for the years to come, with plenty of good times ahead of us.

Looking back, 'A' still sounds very good to me!!

Thank you Jacques, for giving us the chance to choose on that day.

Luc Bellefeuille

"He wrote a good one, eh?" Jacques said when Joe finished.

Joe nodded. "There's this tradition that's such a big part of this place. You celebrate your successes not just when they happen, but ongoing too."

Jacques nodded, "That can only happen when you have elders in your tribe. People who have been around for a long time. When everyone cycles in and out every couple of years, tradition means nothing."

"This is really impressive," Joe said and pointed to a section of the email he had just read. "In less than four years, people had earned through their bonuses, more than they would have gotten if they had taken the buyout."

Jacques nodded, "And they keep getting bonuses because they're still here. Which I can pretty much guarantee you wouldn't have been the case for everyone if we had taken the offer."

"Why is that?"

"Most buyouts happen because someone is doing something well and someone else wants that too. Only the buyer typically gets so caught up in the numbers, policies, internal politics, jockeying for position, and all the rest of that bullshit, that they destroy the very thing they wanted.

"They don't realize it's the people and the culture which creates the success. The very thing they bought is the first thing they destroy. And all the rest flows downhill too.

"Had we accepted the offer, I guarantee our culture would have gone to hell because they wouldn't have understood things like taking as much vacation time as you need. Then, because of some claim about redundancy or overlapping responsibilities, or because they didn't understand the way we use our R&D lever to keep things running on an even keel without undue stress, they'd have fired twenty percent of the DLGL people."

He shrugged, "Pretty soon it would have been all gone."

Jacques paused, then chuckled, "And for those who would have received enough to retire…. Well, the idea of retiring is a bit of a misnomer when you already like what you're doing. You're going to do *something* every day when you get up. And ideally, it's something you like.

"I'm not saying no one here would do anything different if they won the lottery and never had to think about money again. The goal for DLGL though, was to create a place where people *wanted* to be every Monday morning. Including me.

"The buyout offer was nice to get. At the end of the day though, I wasn't trying to escape from a bad situation to then go finally live my dream life and have fun hanging out with people I like. I already have that at DLGL."

He shrugged, "And I think you'd get a similar answer if you talked to most of the other people here."

Chapter 60

"DO YOU MIND GIVING ME THE OVERVIEW OF WHAT OPSCOM is?" Joe asked. "You've referenced it during some of our earlier talks, and it's here again in that email we were just discussing."

"I've had it on my list of things to ask you about and just hadn't gotten to it yet. Since I'm about to sit in on my first OPSCOM meeting, I'd like to know a little of the history and purpose behind it if you don't mind."

Jacques nodded, "OPSCOM came about because of what happened with Claude. Once he got sick, we realized we needed to re-think how we managed the company. Claude was getting close to retiring from daily activities at DLGL, and so something was going to change whether we wanted it to or not.

"Because before that, I'd just walk into his office and put my feet up on his desk and say we have *this* problem, or *that* issue, or *that* opportunity. And he'd do the same type of thing. A lot of it was done on that little wrought iron bench alongside the river that I mentioned before.

"So we'd have our discussions and make all the decisions like that. Bringing in whoever was pertinent to the subject at hand. It was informal. The executive power sat with the two of us. Sort of like a two-headed CEO.

"When he learned he was ill, we said we need to work on spreading this to other people. So we picked four of our most experienced people to join Claude and I. Then eventually, Claude stopped coming, so it was just five of us."

Joe nodded, "Why that number?"

Jacques shrugged, "We like to keep meetings to the lowest possible number of participants while still getting the job done. With the group we picked, there are two people from client operations. They represent what we're doing day to day. Then one from business architecture, which is where our product is going business-wise as we look forward. Another is a person involved with the tools, people, and operational aspects of DLGL daily operations. And then me."

Jacques paused for a moment, "Keep in mind though Joe, that there is considerable overlap among all of us. It's not a series of chiefs coming in to report on their specific domain. Everyone is involved in each other's area. So these meetings are wide-open discussions of everything that's going on."

Joe nodded, "So before the OPSCOM group was formed, the meetings between you and Claude were pretty informal and occurred whenever they needed to. Is that the same way it is now, just with the OPSCOM group?"

Jacques shook his head, "No. Our approach and our philosophy toward this meeting is that it's probably the most important thing we do every week. In a lot of other organizations I've interacted with, you try to minimize the amount of time you spend in meetings, because for the most part, they're unproductive ways to fill the day. OPSCOM is very different.

"We have a simple, straightforward, and fixed agenda. Every week we review every single client. What's going on with them, what activities are happening, the state of our relationship....

"We also talk about which of our products and services they use now and which they could use. And lastly, we discuss any internal issues in terms of how having this client is impacting the people at DLGL."

Joe looked at Jacques quizzically, "For example?"

"For example, if there's a new person who comes into the client organization who decides one of our people should be working at ten o'clock at night to solve their issues. That's not tolerated."

"Got it."

"We take as much time as necessary to review these things in detail. To make sure everything is aligned in the right way. And because we have these conversations every week, if any adjustments need to be made, or any interventions need to happen, we can do it right away.

"This keeps us from having a situation where something goes undiscovered for a month. Then unaddressed for another month. Then by the time someone's actually looking into it, it's a huge issue. That doesn't happen here. We identify it, figure out what needs to be done, and then take action right away."

Joe nodded, "What about the decision making process? Do you vote? How do things get decided?"

Jacques laughed, "Through *very* animated discussions. Every one of the five people in OPSCOM has *distinct opinions* on certain things. So it leads to some incredibly animated conversations.

"And that's good. It's very good. Actually I think that's why OPSCOM is so successful and why in turn, DLGL is so successful. No one in those meetings is afraid of being fired or feeling the need to impress each other. We're not jockeying for position for who is going to get promoted to the next big role.

"Because of that, we're not afraid to bring up our opinions. We're not afraid to have very lively conversation on topics. I mean if something's important, you should really explore it from all different angles, and that's what we do with our format."

Jacques looked at Joe, "I love when the discussions get spirited. Do you know why?"

Joe smiled, "Why?"

"Because it means people care. They have moral ownership of what's going on."

"Moral ownership?"

"Uh-huh. It's fine to have financial ownership. It's important and we do it here. People get rewarded through their salaries and bonuses. When the company does well, they do well. But that by itself would fall apart when times got tough. Because it only drives people to a certain extent.

"Far more powerful is moral ownership. That's when people deeply and genuinely care because they take pride in what they do. They are the guardians of something important.

"It's like the difference between an army of paid mercenaries and an army made up of volunteer civilians who are defending their homes. The civilians are people who live in that country. Their families are there. Their memories, histories, attachments….all there. They will die for those things."

Jacques laughed, "We're not putting people in positions where they need to fight off invaders. But our culture is such that people will fight for what's right at DLGL because of the morale ownership they feel. They helped build this place. They *are* this place. The memories, history and attachments all exist."

Joe nodded, "I've never heard the term moral ownership before. I've definitely seen the same spirit though. Every great company I've ever been in has had it. Every great leader I've ever interviewed, helped build it within their organization."

"There's another important aspect to our method of making decisions," Jacques said. "By the time we make the decision, everyone is supportive of it. We might have arrived by different means, or different parts of the conversation, but we're all there."

"Are the five original members still the same ones on OPSCOM?" Joe asked.

Jacques nodded, "They are." He smiled, "We've been using this format for a long time. It's been one of the keys to our success so far and will continue to be going forward."

Chapter 61

JOE AND JACQUES CHATTED FOR A FEW MORE minutes. Then one by one the OPSCOM participants came into the conference room. Joe had met all of them at one time or another during his days at DLGL. This was the first time he'd sat in on a meeting with all of them though.

When everyone had arrived, Jacques re-introduced Joe to the group. "And Joe," he said. "One of the keys to a great OPSCOM meeting is that there's no such thing as a passive observer. I know you haven't spent all that much time here at DLGL. Still, if you've got something to add, by all means, jump in. Everyone here is a participant."

Joe smiled. Jacques comment was almost exactly the same one he'd heard Thomas say so many times to people who came to events at Derale Enterprises. As Joe reflected on that, he realized something. The thought hadn't triggered the darkness he'd been feeling the last seven months when memories of Thomas would cross his mind. A part of Joe wanted to process that further, but the meeting was already kicking off.

As Jacques had explained, the group took it client by client. Joe noticed that the clients were assigned a color, depending on the state of the relationship. Green meant everything was great. Yellow meant there was some uneasiness in the relationship. Red meant there was a crisis with the client.

Blue meant everything was frozen. The clients was using VIP, DLGL's product, but no evolution was expected right now because of internal policies, or other factors.

And lastly, there was brown. A client who was coded brown would receive one hundred percent of the support, tools, and other items in their contract. Just like any other client. However, DLGL would not look to expand the relationship with them. The primary reason for a client getting a brown color was because they had become disrespectful to the people at DLGL and were trying to create stress.

As Jacques explained to Joe when they came to a brown client, "It's just not tolerated. As an organization, we're very competent and we try very hard. If that's not enough, we'll talk about it and try to find solutions. If after all that it's still not enough, we won't work with them on additional projects.

"The idea that the customer is always right is bullshit. The *collective* customer is right. A single customer represented by a single individual at a given point in time…. Who doesn't understand what they're doing and is trying to make a name for themselves, or redirect their incompetencies to someone at DLGL…. Is definitely not right.

"We constantly go back to—'What is in the best long-term interest of the client?' The current client person may not like something. But in three years, *or less*, they'll probably be gone. That happens a lot. But we'll still have to explain *our* side of the story. Why we recommended something.

"And the answer has to be a lot better than—because that guy who you have since fired, was ranting and raving and *made* us do it.

"The goal is lots of Green clients and a low number of anything else. The energy we spend on Red clients is frightening. That time could be so better spent. So the goal is to keep them out of there. Since we meet every week, we can quickly see if someone goes from Green to Yellow and address it before it goes to Red.

"What's the normal breakdown?" Joe asked.

"79% green, 5% yellow, 3-5% red, 10 % blue, and 1-3% brown," Jacques replied.

"And is there a particular reason they tend to move from one color to another?" Joe asked.

Jacques nodded, "A change in who we're dealing with on the client side. Things can go from not good to great by one person being replaced on the client side.

"Or the reverse. Which is the case with this client we're talking about. We had a great relationship with the client person for eighteen years. Then he retired and was replaced by a new person from the outside who doesn't know us and doesn't even know his own business either.

"You get a situation like that, with someone trying to make his mark, justify a bigger budget, build up his resume in a particular area…and it's bad news. The first thing they say is, 'Oh, we've had this system for eighteen years? It must be a legacy system and needs to be replaced.'

"They'll start throwing a bunch of buzz words around trying to get support for making a change."

Jacques shook his head, "This is where the headache comes in. And where we end up investing time which would be better spent elsewhere. Because what the person should be saying is—'Thank goodness I'm walking into a situation where my vendor not only produces great results for us, they've been doing it for so long, they know us really well. Not to mention they continue to upgrade their products to deliver what we need.

"Thank goodness I'm with a vendor who has never missed payroll for any client in the history of their company. Thank goodness all the foundational work is done for our data systems. Because things like mapping out processes, procedures, and administrivia detail, can take five to seven years. Which means for five to seven years everyone would be missing the data they need to effectively run their business.

"Thank goodness my vendor has a product which is up to date, competitive, still winning new business in the marketplace, well supported, and has such a strong culture that their people don't leave. Because that means the people who did the original mapping of processes and procedures and provided ongoing support are still there.

"So when something needs to be developed or adjusted, it's a quick fix. Instead of spending countless hours trying to figure out what was done, only to create workaround after workaround and end up with a patchwork of spaghetti technology."

Joe smiled. One of the things he really enjoyed about Jacques was he told it like it was. And he was also very passionate about what he did. "So why don't they say those things?" Joe asked.

Jacques shook his head, "Don't get me wrong. Most of them do. And in those cases, we're at green and we stay green through the transition to the new person. Perfect. However, in a scenario like this, it's different. The person they hired to replace our previous client counterpart, is more focused on his personal objectives than the objectives of the overall organization he represents.

"So you end up with a guy whose trying to build his resume by saying he's done *this* type of software implementation. Or transitioned to *that* type of technology. Or managed *this* size of a budget. He'll make all kinds of changes, start all kinds of projects, and create a nice mess. Then he'll move on in two or three years before anything is really done, and just before things start to hit the fan."

Joe nodded, "Sounds like what you were sharing the other day. A case of misaligned objectives."

"Exactly," Jacques replied. "For this particular case, eventually someone on the client side realized what this guy was doing and the way he was treating people. So they fired him. But he created enough problems along the way, it has left a mess. If his replacement has a lot better attitude, we'll look to expand the relationship again. If not, then we won't."

Jacques shrugged, "There is a level of arrogance required on our part to know who we are, what we can deliver and where we're going. It allows us to take a stand when necessary. Which is important. Because better to take a stand early when it's not good and clearly won't be good, than to let something like that suck up your time and energy."

Jacques shrugged again, "And it works. Over the years we've continued to add new clients. We've never lost one. And we're ever increasing our relationship with most of them, because we keep looking for new ways to help them be more successful. It's a good arrangement."

Jacques paused, "But…" he began.

"But in the back of your mind, you're thinking about what's going to happen in the future," Joe said. "When more of your original client counterparts retire."

Joe smiled, "Sorry. I didn't mean to interrupt your thoughts. I've just noticed that there's this pattern in what happens here. You do your best to deal with things that *might* become issues—*before* they become issues."

Jacques smiled, "No apology necessary, Joe. You're here as a participant, not just an observer. You're right. By being proactive in these things and catching them before they happen, we avoid a lot of the crisis you see other places.

"In this case, we're dealing with something unique. Not many companies have a situation where they've been with their clients so long, their original client counterparts are retiring."

Joe nodded. He looked around the table at the participants, "I've got an idea for you."

Chapter 62

OVER THE NEXT FIFTEEN MINUTES, JOE MAPPED OUT something he had witnessed at DLGL.

The client names on the conference rooms. The tree with the notes from client people who had spent six months at DLGL during their company's project. The longstanding relationships and friendships that were maintained between support people at DLGL, and the daily users of DLGL's software....

He drew funny parallels between DLGL's client relationships, and a relationship between two people. How at the start there was courting, connection, admiration, romance. That was sort of what happened when the clients spent months working at DLGL. The dedication to building great things, the positive atmosphere, free fruit twice a day, the badminton games, the Vipnasium, the teamwork, the commitment to creating something.

Everyone was in love.

But over time, as people retire or leave from the client side, the strong connection back to DLGL weakens. In relationships, when the connection weakens, people forget how special the other person is. Or they forget how much that other person contributes.

In this situation, the client counterparts might not realize how much DLGL contributes to the success of their business. Or how great they are as a partner. So then when a new potential suitor comes calling, they're more willing to listen than they would have been in the past.

Especially if the new client counterpart is someone who was brought in from the outside. Someone who had nothing to do with the original project work and no connection to DLGL or the VIP product. They weren't part of the team which built together, played together, laughed together. To them, DLGL is just a vendor, and VIP is just a software.

Joe explained the museum day concept and how powerful it would be if each client were able to see their relationship with DLGL in *that* context. To experience fifteen or twenty years of successes, laughter, and achievements. There could be images of people designing, creating, and building together. Quotes, statistics, and more images all showing the impact of their collective efforts over the years.

-Millions of paychecks distributed right on time and exactly to the penny. Paychecks which are the reward for a job well done. And the source for people's mortgage payments, school tuition, family vacations....

-Hundreds of thousands of people scheduled precisely each and every day. Enabling the most important functions within the organization to be completed so that clients could be served effectively and efficiently.

-Millions of queries to the VIP databases each and every day, returning quick and precise numbers so leaders could make key businesses decisions and fulfill their organization's purpose.

Joe discussed how a new person coming into the relationship would understand things better if they were to walk that museum. Either in person, or virtually somehow. They would get a sense of the deep and important connection that existed between DLGL and their company.

He also explained one of the core concepts Thomas had taught him. A concept which Joe had in turn taught countless other leaders through his role at Derale Enterprises. The question was never 'How?' As in, 'How can we...?' The question was always 'Who?' Who has done, seen, or experienced what we want to do, see, or experience?'

"You have a unique challenge on your hands," Joe said as he was summing things up. He smiled, "It's a question of love. What would be an effective way to keep the love going with your existing clients? Even as people retire, the players change, or new suitors keep calling? And what would be an effective way to help new clients fall in love with you too?

"Interestingly enough," Joe continued, "You are your own 'Who'."

Jacques smiled, "In what way, Joe?"

"You design things in ways that they can be used for all your clients, not just one. You understand the importance of building for the long term, not just a quick fix. You're willing to invest up front in your relationships, realizing that although the payment may be down the line, it will far outweigh the upfront investment.

"You know that culture is best transferred through stories. That's what the Big Little Book of Emails is. And perhaps most important, you understand moral ownership—the degree to which people want to be a part of something that matters, and will fight with all they have when someone threatens to take that away."

Joe smiled again, "From my perspective, it's simply a matter of applying those same approaches to the client museum idea."

Chapter 63

IT WAS FIVE-THIRTY. JOE AND JACQUES WERE IN THE car heading to the event Jacques was going to speak at. Following Joe's comments about the client museum, the OPSCOM team had been furiously mapping out ideas. They were still at it when Joe and Jacques left.

"How are you feeling?" Jacques asked.

Joe smiled and nodded, "Good. Very good."

"What you did back there was a pretty impressive piece of work," Jacques commented. "You've been mostly quiet and observing what we do well over these past couple of weeks. I think today we got a better glimpse into what Joe Pogrete does well."

Joe smiled again, "I love that stuff. Connecting the dots. Seeing the patterns and helping put it all together to make something unique and special. Creating."

He laughed, "The actual implementation of it all is not my strength. I know that. But I love helping people dream it up and then seeing the end result."

"Have you ever seen a client museum like what you were proposing?" Jacques asked.

Joe thought for a few minutes, "In Taiwan there's this amazing place called the Hall of Still Thoughts. The context around what they've done is different, but the spirit is certainly similar."

He paused a moment, "When I'm out sharing stories of different great leaders, people often ask me who's the greatest one I've ever come across. It's not really a fair question because each leader has their own path, their own purpose.

"Certainly one of the greatest though, is the woman who inspired the Hall of Still Thoughts. She's a petite little person. Maybe five feet tall and ninety pounds at most. Her name is Master Chen Yen and she's a Buddhist monk in Taiwan."

Jacques chuckled, "Really?"

Joe nodded.

"This sounds like the kind of story I want to hear," Jacques said.

Joe smiled, "She has an amazing life story. Like most great leaders, initially she was searching for her own identity. Who am I? What do I want to do with my life? What is my purpose?

"Her father was very successful, and it would have been easy for her to continue on with the family businesses. But that wasn't her path. She knew it.

"She searched for years, seeking her unique and special place in the world. Eventually she decided she wanted to become a Buddhist monk."

"I didn't know there were female monks," Jacques said.

Joe nodded, "Some. It's not all that common, which is part of what makes her story that much more amazing. After she decided becoming a monk was her path, she met resistance. People tried to give her rules, regulations, and a long list of what had to be done in order for her to 'prove' or 'qualify' to be a monk. To her credit, she saw through that. She knew leading oneself isn't about who someone else says you are. It's about who you know in your heart *you* are.

"She came up with a code for her life. Guidelines, philosophies.... A lot about being responsible for her own situation, making a difference, helping people, and taking action. Others who felt connected to her approach, were free to join her on her adventures if they wished. Which is exactly what happened.

"As she lived her code, she began to attract people. They were drawn to her conviction and her selflessness. And I think in large part too, they were drawn to her because her life philosophy included each person doing their best to take responsibility for their own situation.

"One day she was in a hospital and she noticed there was blood on the floor. She asked someone what had happened. They told her that people had carried a woman for hours from a village in the mountains. The woman was obviously hurt, but the family didn't have the money required to enter the hospital. So she was sent away, still bleeding.

"Master Chen Yen saw this and thought there had to be a better way. So she began raising funds for a hospital. A hospital which would serve all people who were in need. As the funds for the hospital were being raised, she started looking for doctors. Not just any doctors, but doctors who took time with patients, genuinely cared about them, and treated them as human beings.

"She had a hard time finding the calibre of doctor she wanted. So in addition to raising funds for the hospital, she started raising funds for a medical school. A place where new doctors would be trained with the understanding that compassion and connection are every bit as important as medical knowledge.

"Then she realized these challenges existed in the nursing staff as well, so she started a nursing school too. When all that was up and running, she turned her attention to building schools for children, then to preserving the environment, then to disaster relief...."

Jacques chuckled again, "Impressive."

"It is," Joe replied. "The organization she founded is called Tzu Chi. They've done more for people than any other organization I've ever come across. *Anywhere.*

"When hurricanes, floods, earthquakes, or other events happen, they are on the ground, making a difference. In most cases, they are getting food and supplies to people faster than anyone else, including the government agencies who are supposed to handle that.

"They are innovators. For example, they've literally figured out a way to turn the plastic bottles they recycle, into blankets and clothing for their disaster relief efforts. Old TV screens are transformed into beautiful bracelets which are sold to raise money for their education programs....

"Nothing is wasted. Every person who wants to volunteer is found a project. Items which others would throw away, they transform into something useful. It's truly impressive."

Joe shrugged and smiled, "Master Chen Yen has never left Taiwan. Yet there are over ten million people in over forty seven countries who have been inspired enough by her story, her writings, and her efforts, that they volunteer for the Tzu Chi organization. They make a difference literally around the world, all through volunteers."

"How did you come across the organization, and the founder?" Jacques asked.

"I was in Taiwan, speaking. Part of what I shared was the Big Five for Life and the concept of Museum Day. There were some members of Tzu Chi in the audience and they invited me to visit the place I mentioned earlier—The Hall of Still Thoughts. They thought I would enjoy it because of the connection to what I'd been presenting. And I have to tell you, the hall is amazing."

"In what way?"

"Part of it is its beauty. Usually I'm not the type of person who notices details. I don't care what table I sit at in a restaurant. I don't really notice the color of something.

"Well, even for someone like me, this place stood out. Every detail is perfect. The look of the wood flooring, the layout, the way the displays in the hall are designed. It's beautiful, and calming, and inspiring all at the same time. It's also massive.

"They have special exhibit areas dedicated to the different focuses of the organization. Education, the environment, health.... Then within each section, are examples of the projects they've done and the impact they've had.

"It is the kind of place which inspires you in ways you never thought you would feel inspired. It reminds you of your true potential as a human, and also of our collective potential to make a difference."

Joe smiled, "As you walk through, you find yourself being more and more impressed at what the organization has accomplished. And I also couldn't help but marvel at the way they put all the exhibits together."

"How so?" Jacques asked.

"People make decisions with this interesting blend of emotion and logic. Usually they act on emotion and justify with logic. The exhibits blend those two really well.

"On the emotional side are all these photos and stories, which make it personal, real, and fun. So you might see pictures of a group of volunteers giving food and blankets to survivors of a tsunami. Or images of people laughing together as they help build schools, or collect recyclables.

"Along with the pictures are write-ups. They explain what inspired the actual volunteers in the picture to help out. Also what contribution they've made. The way it's done, makes it very personal. Something which as a visitor, you really connect to.

"Supporting all the pictures and stories are charts and data which show the sheer impact of what *all* the volunteers have accomplished. I don't remember the exact numbers, but it would be things like—31,450 blankets distributed in three days to those impacted by a tsunami.

"Another sign would say something like—over three million plastic bottles collected and recycled in two months."

Joe shrugged, "The hall is this perfect blend of environment, stories, and impact. When you get done walking through it, the overarching feeling you have is you want to be a part of what's going on there. You want to help.

"I was told that executives have quit their jobs on the spot and volunteered full time for the organization. People have become so overcome with a sense of connection that they contribute in whatever way they can. In some cases through financial contributions. In other cases by volunteering resources from their companies.

"It's a place which inspires people because they see that great things get done there. Really wonderful things. Meaningful things. And people want to be a part of that."

Joe turned to Jacques, "In general, I think people want to do something meaningful with their lives. They want to be a part of something good. But they are much more likely to join something which exists, than to start it on their own. So this place, this organization, gives them that opportunity."

"All led by a petite, female Buddhist monk," Jacques said.

Joe nodded, "This woman is a force of nature for good. And on top of that, she understands processes, motivation, innovation, and connecting with people, like very few in the world."

He smiled, "There are definitely many really great leaders out there. Including you, Jacques. And not every leader is right for every person because of their styles, beliefs, or what they're working on.

"For me, this lady has always stood out as an incredible example of the impact a positively focused leader can have. So the answer to your question, which is what started this whole conversation, is yes. The Hall of Still Thoughts is a *great* example of a leader creating a museum which inspires people to new levels of connectedness with what an organization does and why."

"Sounds like a great 'Who,'" Jacques said.

Joe nodded, "A very great one."

Chapter 64

JOE AND JACQUES ARRIVED AT THE EVENT LOCATION a little before six o'clock. They were immediately greeted by one of the event hosts.

"So nice to have you here, Jacques. Thank you very much for coming. My name is Marguerite."

Jacques shook her hand, "Nice to meet you in person, Marguerite. Thanks for inviting me." He turned toward Joe, "This is Joe Pogrete. He's the friend I mentioned I'd be bringing with."

Joe and Marguerite shook hands and exchanged pleasantries.

"Let's get you settled," Marguerite said. "We'll be starting in about thirty minutes. There are two speakers tonight. You, Jacques, and a gentleman from a very high profile recruiting agency. You'll both be talking on the same subject—how to attract the best talent. Specifically individuals in the Generation X and Generation Y category.

"As we discussed through our emails, it would be wonderful if you could present your perspective on what those candidates are looking for. The types of jobs, the types of companies, the types of employers.... The people in the audience tonight are CEO's of some of the largest organizations in the province. Some private, others public."

"Also, at each table we have one person between thirty to thirty-five years old, who has been noted as a high performer in the province. A fast tracker at their company."

Jacques nodded, "I can't say I'll be able to talk about anyone else's organization, but I'll certainly share what we see at DLGL."

Marguerite patted Jacques on the shoulder, "Since your company has won the best place to work in the province the last thirteen years, and best in Canada twice, including this year, I'm sure people will be very interested in what you have to say."

The room had about a dozen large circular tables in it. Marguerite showed them to one in the front where they'd be sitting.

"The technician will be right over to get you a body microphone. And then we'll be getting started in just a little while," she said. "Is there anything else you need?"

Jacques shook his head, "Nope, I think we're all set."

* * *

At promptly six-thirty, Marguerite opened the evening with some introductory remarks. Then she turned the floor over to the other speaker, who began his presentation. As Marguerite had said, he was with a high-end recruiting and headhunter agency.

It took just a few minutes for Joe to realize it was going to be an evening of opposite opinions. The first speaker's assessment was that high performers in the Generation X and Generation Y age brackets were looking for mobility. They wanted to spend two years somewhere and then move on to a different company.

"This is the present, and this is the future," he said. "Companies need to adapt to this and learn to live with it. Don't expect these candidates to have more of a link with a company than those two years. They are there to have a job, learn what they can, and then leave to pursue other interests."

He went on for about fifteen minutes more, citing multi-tasking desires, the need for constant stimulation, the amount of times people checked their smart phones every day....

Joe glanced at Jacques. He shrugged.

Chapter 65

WHEN THE FIRST SPEAKER WAS DONE, MARGUERITE introduced Jacques and he went up on the stage.

Jacques paused for a moment as he stood and looked out at the audience.

Joe smiled to himself. He had a friend who had grown up in a very rural area. This friend would often open discussions with the demeanor of a small town, country guy. Very unassuming. Very self-deprecating. Not flashy at all.

Then he would start dropping in details, statistics, key information points. And before long, people realized they were in the presence of someone who was ridiculously smart. Joe had a hunch that many of the audience members were going to go through that same experience over the next few minutes.

Jacques looked out at the audience for a moment more and then began, "You know, I want to thank our first speaker for his presentation. I very much enjoy hearing the opinions of others on different topics. It helps me think through my own beliefs and perspectives. And of course everyone's reality is based on what they see going on around them."

Jacques nodded his head toward the other speaker, "So thank you for sharing what you did." Jacques paused for a moment again, "I have to apologize though, because based on my experiences at DLGL...I completely disagree with you."

Joe smiled.

"A lot of what you were describing may *be* the attitude of people," Jacques began. "But it's not what they prefer. It is a reaction to the fact that *corporations* are not being loyal. How do you expect people to be loyal to an employer, when it is clearly not reciprocated?

"The truth is, people *are* available to be loyal. And in the right environment, they *will* stay longer than two years. As a matter of fact, in the right environment, they'll stay for their whole career.

"The problem lies in the corporations and the way they're treating their people. They're not paying attention. They're not doing what they need to do. And therefore, they're creating their own problems."

Jacques paused for a moment and let that sink in, "The cost of replacing your best people is very high. At the two year mark, you've got someone who has really just started to be optimally efficient. They've learned the ropes a bit, mastered some of the internal dynamics, are familiar with the market, the industry.... And then you lose them and have to start all over?

"That's an incredibly expensive process. It's not sustainable in the long term. So instead of pretending it's something we all have to live with, I suggest you fight it.

"How do you do that? First of all, admit that the problem is with the company, not the employees. Then start demonstrating loyalty to the employees and they will pay it back in kind."

Jacques shrugged, "When Marguerite contacted me about speaking tonight, I told her I wasn't sure I was the guy she wanted. At

DLGL we don't recruit people. We have a zero percent turnover rate and the average tenure of our employees is sixteen years. So we don't have to be out there trying to get a bunch of new people every year.

"The ones we do hire, are from a pool of individuals who sought us out because of the way we operate, and our reputation for treating people well. They are top performers looking for a better environment in which to use their talents.

"Although we don't add a lot of people all the time, we do grow. But our growth comes from constantly improving what we do. When good people stay, they keep getting smarter and more efficient. So you end up helping more clients, and growing your business, without needing to grow your employee base.

"So our focus isn't on recruiting new talent. It's on making sure our existing talented people are happy where they are."

Jacques looked toward where Marguerite was sitting and smiled, "But Marguerite said she understood all that, and that was the information she wanted me to present. So here I am."

He shrugged, "I like to keep life pretty simple. So I've broken things down into just a few main thoughts for tonight."

Chapter 66

A PRESENTATION SLIDE APPEARED ON THE SCREEN behind Jacques. There were four points.

DLGL

Corporate Culture

Our HR Practices

Commitment

Jacques pressed a button and the slide disappeared, "DLGL is a specialized company," he began. "We started thirty-two years ago and we specialize in the creation and long-term support of human resource systems for the largest businesses across Canada. We also serve some American customers who are affiliated with our Canadian customers. As a frame of reference, our expertise and focus puts us in direct competition with companies like SAP, PeopleSoft, and Oracle."

Jacques paused for a moment, "In terms of our corporate culture, I believe DLGL's secret is we have a high degree of respect for people right from the start. We are driven by a clear philosophy, which is to provide a high quality of life for all the people in our business. That applies to employees, customers and the shareholders.

"Having competent and happy employees allows us to deliver products and services that are absolutely extraordinary. That's how we succeed in being a leading competitor, despite our comparatively very small size.

"The value is delivered to the employees, then it is delivered to the customers. Consequently, at the end of the line, there is a value for the shareholders.

"This is the reverse of what is done in many places. There, the starting point of their efforts is to create value for the shareholders by squeezing everything they can from the employees and customers."

Jacques paused again and looked around the room, "In my opinion, this inversion of the value proposition that we do—is our greatest secret.

"Do we want good contracts? Absolutely. Do we want profitable contracts? Absolutely. However, unlike in organizations where growth is the objective at all costs—our growth doesn't come from signing questionable contracts just to hit a number.

"We have always delivered with a 100% satisfaction. Part of that is because of our approach to clients. We insist on customers who are pleasant to work with. We don't take ones who will probably treat our people poorly. And we don't keep ones who *prove* they will treat our people poorly.

"By focusing on our employees, who then focus on our customers, we do things well. Because of that we get growth. And it's the kind of growth we want."

Jacques hit a button and a new slide appeared—HR Inspiring Practices.

He looked out at the audience, "Over the years, we have put things in place to make our people's lives comfortable. For example, we distribute fruit, nuts, and other healthy food options to everyone in the company, twice a day. It's all free. We used to have vending machines. They provided an enormous amount of chocolate, coffee, and other not so healthy foods to our people.

"So we decided to switch. People in good mental shape make better decisions. Sitting on a caffein buzz or sugar high isn't the place from which to make good decisions.

"People in good physical health also make better decisions. So for that reason we have installed two gymnasiums for our people. One is for basketball, volleyball, badminton.... The other we call the Vipnasium. It is a first class training facility for all kinds of sports.

"The point of having all this on site is it facilitates people using it. No one has to drive forty-five minutes to get to their gym. It's just a few floors above them and is as state of the art as any gym they could join. They can use any of these facilities, and others we have, any time they want during the day.

"They have their own lockers where they can leave clothes for after they exercise. Towels are provided by a towel service. All of these conveniences are part of the way we contribute to the balance in our people's lives."

Jacques flipped the slide once more—Commitment

He paused for a moment, deciding how to say what he wanted, "I absolutely do *not* believe in the theory that the new generation wishes to make two year internships everywhere across the country as they continually change jobs. It's not always the best thing to put your children in another school every two years. Or sell your house every two years. Or start over in a new city and have to make new friends and new connections—every two years.

"I *am* convinced that the new generation of people that are often called 'not loyal' seem to be reacting that way because businesses are not loyal. The truth is, people want to find a place where they can pursue a rewarding and stimulating professional life.

"And that doesn't mean they should have to work seventy hours a week just to keep their job or be viewed as a 'high performer'. When you work that much, you have no social life and you have no family life. That's not life. We would never ask that in any way of our people.

"Our philosophy I mentioned earlier, of focusing on reasonable contracts and reasonable customers, is in large part what allows us to have reasonable deadlines. Because we have those, people work thirty-five to thirty-seven hours per week instead of seventy. If we come across someone who absolutely needs to work seventy hours a week, we suggest they go to one of our competitors, who are more than happy to work them to death.

"Currently there are eighty-seven people at DLGL. They are the same ones who were there five years ago. In an environment with a typical turnover rate of fifteen to twenty percent, it would take three to four hundred people to generate the same throughput as our current eighty-seven. Plus, we certainly wouldn't have the same relationship with our customers.

"We compete in a high-tech industry against organizations five *hundred* times our size. We also address the most organizationally and technologically challenging segment of the market—very large employers. That means each time we talk to a potential client, we need to prove what we do and what we bring to the table.

"Otherwise they will go with one of our jumbo competitors. Because it's easy to pick a company whose name you see on giant lighted signs every forty feet as you walk through the airport. Rarely does someone get fired for that.

"But despite these challenges, we not only survive, but thrive. When a potential client compares us to the competition, they do twelve months of due diligence. That involves analysis by external experts along with six to ten internal specialists. It also involves reviewing our responses to thousands of questions, scenarios we demo, examples from existing clients.... And when all that is complete, *we* win the job.

"We are the best in the world at what we do, and we even push our luck to the point of refusing to grow rapidly as many would want us to.

"All of this is possible because of the products we create and the way in which we do business. And I reiterate again, the starting point for *all* of that, is the way we treat our people."

Jacques looked out across the audience, "As leaders of our respective companies, you and I are making decisions every day. I'll close tonight by sharing with you a pretty basic approach which has served me well in this regard. For finding good people, good clients, and a lot of other things too.

"In my office, are three specific pictures which look back at me every day. I've got others too, but these three are the ones who look right at me. They are Claude Lalonde, the man who founded DLGL with me over thirty years ago. My dog Choco, who was my constant companion for the last fifteen years. And lastly, my Dad.

"They've all passed on. But their spirit has not. And certainly all they taught me has not gone either. Each time I make a decision I ask myself a very simple question-What would they think of what I'm doing right now?

"And if the answer isn't that they'd be proud of me, I know it's the wrong decision."

Jacques nodded toward the audience, "Have a wonderful night."

Chapter 67

WHEN THE EVENT FINISHED, JOE AND JACQUES headed back to DLGL so Joe could get his car.

"What did you think?" Joe asked him as they began driving.

"I don't think that group will be inviting us back," he said and smiled. "I was watching the audience. With the exception of the fast trackers, and a few of the leaders, it wasn't the message they were looking for."

He shook his head, "They were looking for validation on what they already believe. That it's OK to have 15-20% turnover each year. It's good leadership when you can get your people to work from nine in the morning until nine at night. They see themselves as successful. The leaders of huge corporations. Eighteen thousand, twenty thousand people.... From their perspective, they've made it. They don't really want to hear the kind of things we're doing."

He shrugged, "So be it."

Joe nodded silently. He could tell it annoyed Jacques a little. Not because he needed validation for what he'd helped create at DLGL. But because the very people who needed to listen, weren't. And a lot of people would suffer because of that.

"You remember during the Q&A at the end, when that group of young fast trackers were talking about a particular company who has a tough time recruiting?" Jacques asked. "They didn't name the organization, but I know who it is. They are legendary in our industry for the way they treat people—and for all the wrong reasons.

"They show them no respect. People are treated like a dispensable commodity. They send them all over the place, constantly asking them to pick up their families and move." He shook his head, "They treat employees like pawns in a chess game."

"What did you think of the guy from the trucking industry?" Joe asked.

"You mean the one who kept saying if his female employees in the U.S. knew of the maternity leave benefits here, they'd be jealous. So people here should be more grateful?" Jacques shook his head, "He doesn't get it. He's positioning it as a war between employee and employer. People have too much already…. They should just be grateful…." Jacques shook his head again, "He just doesn't get it."

"Well the fast trackers sure got it," Joe replied. "And agreed with it. I didn't count, but it seemed like every single one of them came up to you afterwards to tell you they agreed with what you said in your presentation."

Jacques nodded, "I hope they find leaders and organizations who treat them right."

As they pulled up to a red light at an intersection, Jacques' phone began to beep. He glanced at it and smiled, "On to happier topics. The OPSCOM team texted me earlier in the evening. They said we should check our email."

"Hang on. I'll pull it up since you're driving," Joe replied. He grabbed his phone and waited while his emails updated. In a moment, the one from OPSCOM was on his screen and he was scrolling through it.

"Well?" Jacques asked.

Joe smiled, "They were busy after we left."

In addition to the idea of creating actual and virtual museums to celebrate individual clients, the team had come up with some 'quick hit' ideas for keeping clients connected to the impact of their collaborative efforts. One of them was writing very brief, but powerful examples which could be added to people's signature line at DLGL.

"It's the signature line idea," Joe said. "Here's a few of them."

FGL Sports, Canada's largest national sporting goods retailer and a DLGL client for 20 years, has expanded its V.I.P. usage across 23 recently acquired stores.

More than 15 years of partnership. Laurentian Bank, which employs 4,500 people, selects DLGL and V.I.P. for their e-Recruitment replacement of Taleo. "They are good partners that we can count on," states Executive Vice-President Corporate Affairs and Human Resources.

New tools now live for 9,000 employees at Regina Qu'Appelle Health Region. (V.I.P. Talent Management, Manager Portal Workbench and MyCareer. Record time delivery. Under budget.)

"This is pretty cool," Joe said as he played with the messages on his screen. "Not only did they create the text, but they made it so every signature line is linked. When you click on the link, it takes you to the DLGL website and you get more information about each of the projects."

"It's a great start," Jacques said and nodded. "Building the love, eh Joe?"

Joe smiled again, "Building the love."

He was about to put his phone away, when he saw that one of his other emails was from Kerry Dobsin. The subject line was—Can you help?

Joe hesitated for a moment, then opened the message.

Chapter 68

AS JOE WAS READING, JACQUES GLANCED OVER. HE could see the change in Joe's demeanor. "Everything OK?"

Joe hesitated for a moment, then nodded and put his phone away, "I had another message waiting for me. It was from one of the board members at Derale Enterprises. They're asking me to come back and present at one of our leadership forums in two weeks."

Jacques nodded, "And?"

"Well, in a sense it's not that surprising. This is the type of thing I do all the time. In this case though, I think maybe there's more to it. There are probably a half-dozen people who could comfortably give the presentation and who are already in town. But they still asked me."

"Why is that?"

"I think this is sort of the big test. They need an answer about the position I mentioned to you before—someone to take over for Thomas." Joe paused for a moment, "I think they want to make sure I'm..." He hesitated.

"Normal?" Jacques asked.

Joe nodded, "Normal."

"Have you ever been normal?" Jacques asked with a smile.

Joe smiled too. It was exactly the type of comment Thomas would have made. And probably the same type of exchange Claude and Jacques would have had too.

"Never," he replied.

Jacques chuckled.

"What do you think you're going to do?" Jacques asked?

Joe thought for a moment, "I don't know."

The two men sat in silence for a few minutes.

"You know, Joe, one of most important things I ever learned about leadership was that I didn't always have to know."

"What do you mean?"

"When I was younger, I thought the leader was the one who knew it all. That's why they were the leader. I started playing hockey when I was about four, and when you're a kid playing hockey, the coach is the leader. They're the one giving all the instructions and coaching people on what to do. So you grow up thinking the leader knows it all.

"But it's not true. And I bet if you were to think about all the great leaders you've interacted with, you'd see it with them too. The really great leaders, and the most successful ones, know they don't need to know everything. They also know they can't be the one who *does* everything.

"They just need to do *their* part, and enable the people around them to do the same." Jacques paused, "That's how you succeed as a leader."

The two men sat in silence for a few moments, then Jacques glanced at Joe, "For what it's worth, Joe, if you decide to take that job…I think you'll be great at it. And if you take the pressure off yourself, and just do what you do well, and enable others to do what they do well…you'll have a hell of a lot of fun at it too."

Chapter 69

JOE WAS STANDING BACKSTAGE OFF TO THE SIDE. HE could see the audience but they couldn't see him. It was a full crowd. He recognized a number of people. Some were leaders within the different Derale Enterprises companies. Others were customers, suppliers, and partners.

He could hear the music playing. It was a mix of energetic and uplifting songs. Joe knew them well. He had picked them out a couple of years back and always used them as the lead-in at events where he was speaking.

He heard a sound behind him and turned around.

"Hello, Joe."

He smiled, "Hi, Maggie."

They hugged each other for a few moments. "All set?" Maggie asked when they separated.

Joe nodded, "All set."

Maggie looked out at the audience, "There's a special guest for you here today," she said. "Third row, near the center."

Joe glanced out and scanned the crowd. It took him a minute, and then he saw who Maggie was talking about. It was Jacques. He was conversing with the person in the seat next to him. Joe smiled.

"He called me and asked if he could be here," Maggie said. "I didn't think you'd mind."

Joe shook his head, "Not at all."

For a moment, they stood in silence. Then Maggie looked up at Joe, "Thank you for what you sent me. About the bright lights. And for the other things you wrote too. It all meant a lot to me."

Joe nodded, "You're welcome, Maggie."

She reached out and hugged him again, then leaned up and kissed him on the cheek. "Have fun out there," she said when she pulled away. "We'll be cheering for you."

Joe smiled, "Thanks."

When Maggie had disappeared out of sight, Joe glanced out at the audience once again. Then he looked at his watch. "It's time," he said.

A few moments later, the lights in the auditorium went dark. Two spotlights clicked on, illuminating the stage. The music that had been playing, faded to quiet. Joe took a deep breath, exhaled, and walked into the light.

For the first thirty minutes of his presentation, Joe covered material he had long ago become familiar with. An introduction to the Museum Day Concept. An overview of the Big Five for Life and the way it was used throughout Derale Enterprises. A few examples showing how people's personal Big Five for Life were ideally intertwined with the way they spent their time at work each day....

When he had finished, he took a moment and paused, looking out over the audience. "Ladies and gentleman, as you know, the goal of these events is to share some of what we discover through the different interviews we do with leaders such as yourselves. Individuals who are making a difference in the lives of their people, and leading successful companies because of it.

"I'd like to spend the next thirty minutes giving you a brief overview of an amazing company I've had the privilege to spend the last few weeks at, and the amazing person who leads it."

Piece by piece, Joe covered the highlights of what he had experienced at DLGL. He gave examples, he told stories, he helped connect it all to specific things the leaders in the audience could do in their own organizations.

It was a great presentation. Sharp, clear, inspiring, useful. The audience loved it.

From her seat in the third row, next to Jacques, Maggie was watching Joe. As she had almost two months earlier, she was looking for something. Not the obvious. He was always a good presenter. Like before, she was looking for that something else. An indicator which would tell her if he was OK or not.

Joe gave his final remarks. When he was done, the people in the audience responded with tremendous applause. He waited a few minutes until the clapping died down, and then gazed out at the crowd.

"We have time for about three questions," he said. "Does anyone have anything they'd like to ask?"

A number of people immediately raised their hands. Joe called on one of them. The person asked how a company goes about finding its purpose and Big Five for Life. Joe took a few minutes and explained the process and provided the name of a resource within Derale Enterprises who could give further help.

"Any other questions?" he asked when he was done.

More hands went up. Joe called on a woman in the back. She asked for more specifics about the PEC used by DLGL.

When Joe finished answering her, he glanced at his watch and smiled, "We have time for one more question." He scanned the audience. There were a lot of hands up. He selected a gentleman near the front.

It took a few minutes for the crew to get a microphone to him. Eventually they did and he turned and faced the stage. "Joe, my question is about Thomas Derale," he began.

Maggie was sitting in her seat next to Jacques. When she heard the start of the man's question, she instinctively grabbed Jacques arm and held it tight. This was where things had gone wrong last time. The presentation had been great, the questions had been fine…. But when someone in the audience had asked about Thomas, that was where Joe had trouble.

"What I'm wondering," the man with the microphone continued, "is who is going to replace him? And when is that going to happen?"

For Joe, up on the stage, it felt like time went into slow motion, then stopped. He heard the man's questions. He felt his mind processing them. Then it was like he was in a state of nothingness.

It was completely quiet. No one was moving. The audience began to fade from his sight. He felt darkness start to spread over him. The same sensation which had so often laid claim to his thoughts and emotions ever since Thomas had passed away.

Chapter 70

AS JOE STOOD ON THE STAGE, FROM A DISTANT recess of his mind, images began to appear. They were of the many conversations he'd had with Jacques over the last few weeks. His mind was searching. Looking for a particular conversation.

For what seemed like an eternity, his mind did nothing but search. Then, just when Joe began to feel a sense of panic, it all connected.

He remembered Jacques explaining to pick a particular memory. His favorite one of Thomas. And to re-direct his mind to that memory, whenever the darkness came.

Suddenly, Joe was standing on a train platform. Thomas was there and he was asking Joe the simplest and yet most profound of questions—'Is it a good museum day morning?'

Joe could see it all in his mind. As if it had happened yesterday. It was clear and sharp, and as he recalled that memory, a thousand others flashed before him. They were all the great moments he and Thomas had shared during their friendship.

"Joe?"

Joe blinked.

"Joe?"

He took a slow, smooth breath and filled his body with air. The room started to come alive again. He could hear sounds. He could see the audience.

He looked down into the crowd at the gentleman holding the microphone who had just said his name for the second time. "That's a great question," Joe said. "The perfect one to end our time together."

Joe paused for a moment, looking out over the audience. He took another slow, smooth breath and walked to the center of the stage, getting as close to the audience as he could.

"In life, we are either looking back, standing still, or moving forward," he said quietly. "There are appropriate times for each. There are times when it makes sense to look back and learn from what turned out different than we wanted. There are times when it makes sense to look back and fondly remember that which filled our life in a good way.

"There are also times when it makes sense to stand still. To be quiet. To contemplate. To regain our center and our sense of clarity.

"And the rest of the time, it's about moving forward. Not because we have to. But because we *want* to. We want to climb the ascending life curve we often talk about here."

Joe paused again, his gaze drifting downward. After a few seconds, he looked up. "As many of you know, I've been struggling with moving forward since the death of Thomas Derale, the man who founded Derale Enterprises. Thomas was my mentor. The man I credit with helping me see the infinite potential in life. The man who taught me everything I know about great leadership. And he was also my best friend in the world.

"Nine months ago, when he died, I felt like a part of me died too. I lost my way. I stopped moving forward."

The entire auditorium was completely quiet. All eyes were on Joe. All ears waiting to hear what he would say next.

"This evening I shared a little of what I've learned from Jacques Guénette and his team at DLGL. What I didn't share, is that a number of years ago, Jacques walked this path that I have been on. When *his* best friend and business partner died much too young, just like Thomas did.

"Spending time with Jacques and the other fine people at DLGL, has helped me understand things in a way I haven't been able to since Thomas died. To once again see life in the way I had learned from Thomas, but had forgotten over the last many months."

Joe nodded toward Jacques, "It is a gift for which I will forever be grateful."

He paused again, then looked out at the audience, "What I remembered, is that life is not about trying to hold on to what we have, so we can stay where we are. It's about moving forward. It's about living our Big Five for Life, filling our existence with Museum Day moments, challenging ourselves with things we aren't even sure we're ready for.... And in the process, climbing our ascending life curve.

"And part of that means letting go. Letting go of the need to be perfect. Because nothing is perfect. Things go wrong, people on our teams do things wrong, *we* as leaders do things wrong at times.... That's life.

"Part of it is letting go of our own self doubts. That goes hand in hand with letting go of being perfect. If we are afraid to act until we know for sure it's all going to go perfectly, we'll never act.

"And part of it, is letting go when those close to us pass away. Because we don't honor them, or our own lives, by only standing still or looking back."

Joe looked out at the man with the microphone, who had asked the question. "Whoever takes the role Thomas had, won't replace him. They can't. He founded this company. He built this culture. He created almost everything we talk about in the context of great leadership...."

"What they'll do instead, is they'll bring everything they learned from Thomas, and the best of who *they* are, and they'll do their part. And that will be enough."

Joe paused one more, "During these last weeks, as I have begun to once again move forward with my life, I have been struck by a single overriding sense." Joe smiled, "And an accompanying little phrase which I picked up from a good friend.

"The sense is that what we have in front of us—are incredibly exciting times. For all of us who are a part of Derale Enterprises, for all of you who are our customers and partners. For everyone."

Joe nodded and smiled, "Exciting times," he said again.

Epilogue

AFTER SAYING HIS GOOD-BYES AFTER THE EVENT, Jacques made his way to the airport and caught a flight back to Montreal. When he arrived home, he pulled into the driveway and went inside.

His wife, Diane, was in the kitchen. She heard him come in and went to greet him.

She gave him a hug and a kiss. "How was it?" she asked.

He hugged her back. A little extra longer than usual. "It was good. He's going to be OK." He smiled and released her, "Better than OK. Much better."

She reached up and touched his cheek. After all these years she knew him well. She could tell he was proud of what had happened and it made her proud of him. She smiled, "I'll make you something," she said and turned toward the kitchen.

Jacques took his things and put them in his office. Then he walked outside and into the backyard. It was a beautiful afternoon. The air was crisp and clean. The sun was just starting to sink in the sky. He walked over to the small, wrought iron bench by the river and sat down. For a while he was silent. Just present to the air, to the smell of the leaves, to the feel of the wind.

"I missed you today, Claude," he said finally. "You'd have enjoyed what happened."

He sat silently again for a few moments, "You should look somebody up. A guy named Thomas Derale. He left here about a year ago." He nodded, "Sounds like the kind of guy who you'd enjoy spending some time with."

Jacques looked out at the waves rippling on the river, "Rub Choco behind the ears for me will you? Tell him I miss him."

After a few moments of sitting in silence, Jacques patted the empty seat next to him and stood up, "Exciting times, my friend," he said. "Exciting times."

Thank you for reading

THE BIG FIVE
for LIFE - Continued

There are many options for you to continue this adventure.

Learn more about DLGL at
www.dlgl.com

Figure out your own Big Five for Life™ at one of our Big Five for Life Discovery courses.

Get help figuring out your organization's purpose and Big Five for Life.

Invite author John P. Strelecky to speak at your organization.

For more information about all of these, please visit:
www.johnpstrelecky.com

About the Author

JOHN P. STRELECKY IS THE #1 BESTSELLING AUTHOR of numerous books, including *The Why Cafe*, *The Big Five for Life* and now *The Big Five for Life - Continued*. He is also the creator of the Big Five for Life concept. His books have been translated into twenty-five languages.

Since their release, The Big Five for Life series of books have inspired both individuals and leaders around the globe. They have been distributed to employees of numerous companies, including IBM, American Express, Boeing, Estee Lauder, and thousands more. They have also been made required reading in university leadership programs around the world.

After receiving many heartfelt requests from readers, John took a year off from writing to create a step-by-step process to enable people to discover their own Big Five for Life. Thousands of individuals around the world have since gone through this life changing experience.

After receiving a similar request from leaders looking to clarify the purpose and Big Five for Life of their organization, John created a step-by-step method for that as well. It has been successfully used by leaders of various sized companies, in a wide variety of industries.

In response to his efforts, John has been honored alongside Oprah Winfrey, Tony Robbins, Stephen R. Covey, and Wayne Dyer, as one of the one hundred most influential thought leaders in the field of leadership and personal development.

When he isn't writing or providing assistance to others, John spends extensive time traveling with his family. Their backpacking adventures have covered more than one hundred thousand miles (almost four times the circumference of the earth).

Additional details about John and the programs and services he offers can be found at:

www.johnpstrelecky.com

Bonus Material

A BIG PART OF THE REASON FOR THE CREATION OF this book was to provide leaders with practical tools to help them lead their own amazing organizations. During the final editing, there were some valuable stories and pieces of information which were cut so the story would flow at the right pace.

However, that material is important and useful, and the thought that it would just disappear, was painful. So instead, it has been made available as a complimentary download.

You can access it at;

www.johnpstrelecky.com/bigfivebonus